WITHDRAWN 3 1526 04013758 7

Project Management Institute

Sidestep Complexity

Project Management for Small- and Medium-sized Organizations

Philip R. Diab, MBA, PMP

D1565269

Library of Congress Cataloging-in-Publication Data

Diab, Philip R.
  Sidestep complexity : project management for small- and medium-sized organizations /
Philip R. Diab.
     p. cm.
  ISBN 978-1-935589-28-0 (alk. paper)
  1. Project management. 2. Small business—Management. I. Title.
  HD69.P75D53 2011
  658.4'04—dc22

                                                                    2011005485

ISBN: 978-1-935589-28-0

Published by: Project Management Institute, Inc.
                       14 Campus Boulevard
                       Newtown Square, Pennsylvania 19073-3299 USA.
                       Phone: +610-356-4600
                       Fax: +610-356-4647
                       E-mail: customercare@pmi.org
                       Internet: www.PMI.org

©2011 Project Management Institute, Inc. All rights reserved.

"PMI", the PMI logo, "PMP", the PMP logo, "PMBOK", "PgMP", "Project
Management Journal", "PM Network", and the PMI Today logo are registered marks of
Project Management Institute, Inc. The Quarter Globe Design is a trademark of the Project
Management Institute, Inc. For a comprehensive list of PMI marks, contact the PMI Legal
Department.

PMI Publications welcomes corrections and comments on its books. Please feel free to send
comments on typographical, formatting, or other errors. Simply make a copy of the relevant
page of the book, mark the error, and send it to: Book Editor, PMI Publications, 14 Campus
Boulevard, Newtown Square, PA 19073-3299 USA.

To inquire about discounts for resale or educational purposes, please contact the PMI
Book Service Center.

                       PMI Book Service Center
                       P.O. Box 932683, Atlanta, GA 31193-2683 USA
                       Phone: 1-866-276-4764 (within the U.S. or Canada) or
                       +1-770-280-4129 (globally)
                       Fax: +1-770-280-4113
                       E-mail: book.orders@pmi.org

Printed in the United States of America. No part of this work may be reproduced or trans-
mitted in any form or by any means, electronic, manual, photocopying, recording, or by any
information storage and retrieval system, without prior written permission of the publisher.

The paper used in this book complies with the Permanent Paper Standard issued by the
National Information Standards Organization (Z39.48—1984).

10 9 8 7 6 5 4 3 2 1

Dedication

To the future of project management, especially
Leila, Victor, and Juliana

Foreword

I have personally known and admired Philip for more than a decade. When I first met him, I was impressed by his wisdom and maturity. Then, a few years later, I found myself serving with him on the PMI Global Board of Directors for the next six years where I observed his intellect, dedication, and commitment to the project management profession. Philip is an excellent, logical thinker who carefully considers all sides of an issue with an open mind. This is illustrated in *Sidestep Complexity* by the breadth of topics and tips provided in an understandable style that is intuitive, fresh, and accessible. This book explains the key elements of project management through analogies, stories, data, and insightful examples based on Philip's personal experience. This is his gift to all of us, particularly those who need a framework that helps to inform leaders in small- and medium-sized organizations of the benefits of project management and how easy it can be to tailor the body of knowledge to meet their unique needs.

He focuses on simplicity and practicality—not taking something complex and simplifying it, but restating it in a way that makes sense to small- and medium-sized organizations. Covering everything from strategic planning, and vision, to the elements and tools needed to execute that strategy through projects, all in light of the "big picture." Philip presents a blueprint of a virtual balanced scorecard. He explains why and the how these elements are important, while providing the reader with many really useful how-to tips on topics from soft skills and leadership to the mechanics of organizing and managing a project.

I think the reader will especially find value in the section on the five attributes of a great project manager—centered on the people, passion for the mission, obsession with excellence, imagining and architecting the future, and focused on delivery. Project managers and organizations that exhibit these qualities are concentrating on all the right things for business and project success.

In a time when some authors are telling us how difficult it is to implement and practice project management, in *Sidestep Complexity*, Philip tells us how simple project management can be. He sets the stage by clearly defining terms and describing the importance of having the right framework and the right talent in the right place.

In *Sidestep Complexity*, Philip conveys a comforting command of *A Guide to the Project Management Body of Knowledge (PMBOK® Guide)* while blending it with valuable interpersonal tips, tempered by pragmatism and humor. He effectively shares ideas and recommendations on best practices to increase the success rate of projects.

It was an honor and a pleasure to write this foreword for Philip's first book. I hope you enjoy it as much as I did.

Karen Tate, MBA, PMP, PMI Fellow   February 2011

Co-author of *The Project Management Memory Jogger, The Advanced Project Management Memory Jogger,* and *The McGraw-Hill 36-Hour Course: Project Management.*

Acknowledgements

I want to take this opportunity to thank the many people who have supported the effort of getting this book written and published. First and foremost my family. I want to acknowledge the effort of my wife and business partner Mary Elizabeth. Her support at work and at home extended above and beyond the call of duty. Her contribution to this book has been critical and included a variety of activities such as brainstorming, copy editing, sound boarding, review, and feedback just to name a few. Special thanks to my parents for their ever vigilant support and never wavering belief in my capabilities. Thank you for being there on the many business trips as a source of support for our family. I want to also acknowledge my kids who have been the source of inspiration for me to strive to do better in my profession.

On the professional front thanks to the many individuals who were kind enough to offer their time in review of the manuscript and offering feedback. Karen Tate, without you this book would have been significantly poorer, your feedback and comments improved the flow of ideas and constructively improved it. Kathy Shawver, Shelly Brotherton, and Al Zeitoun, thank you for the feedback and encouragement that let me know I was on the right track with this endeavor. Thanks to the Project Management Institute community, especially the PMI Board of Directors, for all the learning, knowledge, and networking opportunities that have helped shape/inspire many of the ideas in the book. Thank you also to the folks who have been a direct part of the editing and publishing process, specifically Donn Greenberg, Barbara Walsh, and Dan Goldfischer. Working with you has been a pleasure. I want to also acknowledge Jumana Abdel Aziz whose ability to take my stick drawings and turn them into meaningful, yet elegant graphics is amazing.

I want to also thank Greg Balestrero for being such a wonderful advocate for project management over the past 8 years. Your leadership has dedication to the profession has taken PMI to the next level. More importantly, thank you for your friendship and your continuous support and encouragement.

Finally, I want to also acknowledge the countless mentors, managers, and coaches within the profession who have made it a point to take from their busy schedules to offer their guidance and support throughout my career.

Table of Contents

INTRODUCTION

"The way to get started is to quit
talking and begin doing."

Walt Disney, Founder of Walt Disney Company

The Idea

Shortly after quitting my job in 1996 and enrolling in a full-time MBA program, I happened to be in Boston accompanying my wife at a conference she was attending. While I was in the lobby, I ran into some of the attendees and they talked me into coming to some of the functions. Since I had nothing better to do, I agreed—and the results were fascinating.

The conference was the PMI annual conference that brings together project management practitioners from around the world to share best practices and lessons learned. The aim of PMI was simply to advance the profession of project management.

Project management as a profession at the time was a new discipline in the field of management. While the practice had been around for thousands of years, the emergence of information technology and its transformative power also made project management play a greater role than it had in the past.

One thing that had been apparent from the moment I met these professionals at the PMI conference and has consistently proven true is that project management professionals are different from average business professionals in various industries. They're wired to think differently and work laterally in the organization.

What also struck me about this specific group of people who were attending the leadership meeting portion of the conference is the degree of passion they had for the concepts of project management and the profession as a whole.

That passion was the primary driver that led me to explore a career in project management and seek opportunities to work in a growing field. Ever since, my passion has for project management and how it can be leveraged to help leaders and organizations has continued to grow and expand.

I have seen first-hand how project management can be applied in a diverse set of industries, regional cultures, functions, and organization types. The uniqueness of the body of knowledge and its flexibility makes it extremely easy to adapt and adopt within organizations, regardless of their purposes and aims. From for-profit to governmental, not-for-profit to academic, and public to private organizations, project management has helped shape the business of change and transformation.

Companies like IBM, SAP, Accenture, Bank of America, BAE, Boeing, Citigroup, HP, Deliotte, Oracle, Procter & Gamble, and many more have all come to value project management and attribute their success to its practices.

These giant organizations have all recognized the benefits and the importance of the role of the project manager. One area of business, however, that has not reached this conclusion as quickly and as wide spread is the area of small- and medium-sized business.

Small- and medium-sized businesses have been involved in the profession but not to the extent that is needed. Perhaps some of that can be attributed to the fact that these organizations do not have the resources necessary to adopt project management as quickly as large enterprise organizations.

I recall when I worked at IBM, the company had a dedicated department called the Project Management Center of Excellence which employed a dozen people working on advancing project management in the organization. This department alone is larger than many small companies.

As such, when it comes to translating project management principles found in PMI's *A Guide to the Project Management Body of Knowledge (PMBOK® Guide)* into workable systems, small- and medium-sized organizations have been slower. Some fail to understand the benefits of project management to the organization, while others felt that project management principles simply did not apply.

The idea behind this book is to provide a framework that helps inform leaders in small- and medium-sized organizations of the benefits of project management and how easy it can be to tailor the body of knowledge to meet their unique needs. The focus is on simplicity and practicality of application. It is not that I am attempting to take something complex and simplify it, but rather restate it in a way that perhaps could make more sense to these organizations.

Having worked in organizations of different sizes, shapes, and locations, I hope to apply many of the lessons learned and best practices that I learned in an anecdotal format to help shed some light as to the value of project management to these organizations.

The framework of the book is focused on 10 principles for achieving success in implementing project management in small- and medium-sized organizations. Each of the chapters that follow this introduction will address a key group of lessons learned that together form the foundation for the 10 principles. The principles are:

1. **Know Your Culture:** What impact does the dynamic of corporate culture have on project management?
2. **Get Your Mind Straight:** What is needed to build a healthy environment within the organization to support effective project management activities?
3. **Champion the Vision:** Organizational strategy is important and is linked to effectively implementing project management.
4. **Establish the Buy-in:** There is a need to build support while the organization is implementing project management practices.
5. **Build Unconventional Leadership:** Project management practitioners' role is important to the organization and goes beyond just simple process and methodology.

6. **Master the Basics:** Certain critical success elements need to be implemented in the organization to achieve project success.
7. **Tool Time:** A minimum set of tools are needed to support effective project management in the organization.
8. **Define Success:** What constitutes success on projects? What measures are useful in evaluating success?
9. **Understand Your Stakeholders' Needs:** What do professionals need to do to define the true needs of projects in a manner that ties them to the organization's strategy?
10. **Focus on the Big Picture:** Organizations need to stop worrying about buzzwords and trends like methodologies and focus on simplification.

What's Different?

In order to have a solid understanding of how the principles I identify in this book apply to small- and medium-sized organizations, we have to start with a couple of basic questions. What makes small- and medium-sized organizations different from large sized enterprises?

Before I can answer these questions, I think it would be good to define what small- and medium-sized organizations are.

European member states define small- and medium-sized organizations as enterprises with employees not exceeding 250. The United States, on the other hand, defines these organizations as employing no more than 1,000 for medium-sized ones and 100 for small organizations.

While small- and medium-sized organizations typically have revenue figures that are mere fractions of what large enterprises have, these organizations comprise the majority of businesses worldwide. In the European Union, it is estimated that these organizations comprise 99% of business, and they employ

65 million people. Interestingly, small- and medium-sized business make up 40 to 50 percent of the total GDP worldwide.

All of this points to the simple fact that these organizations are too important to ignore in the focus of advancing project management principles globally and attempting to shape the growth of the profession.

Going back, however, to some of the challenges that are presented to small- and medium-sized businesses, there are several elements that are worth focusing on. They include:

- Access to cash and credit
- Resource and talent availability
- Bandwidth and coverage in middle management
- Dependence on individuals as opposed to systems
- Lack of consistency in performance
- Challenges with professionalism, especially in family-owned businesses
- Lack of clarity on strategy

There are some advantages that small- and medium-sized organizations have that give them greater flexibility and agility in adopting project management. I will explore them further in this book.

Project Management 101

Project management is often seen as a series of complex processes, behaviors, and systems. However, what I came to recognize through years of experience in the field is that simplicity is one of the most important critical success factors. Let me try and paint a picture to help outline what I have come to understand about project management:

Imagine that you are planning a family vacation. As part of this plan, you would have to first consider where this vacation will take place. This plan must be based on your family's likes and dislikes. If, for instance, your children like swimming and spending endless hours at the pool, a beach is a strong contender for the destination of this vacation.

Setting organization strategy is very much like trying to determine the destination of a family vacation. Your organization must establish a vision of "where" you want to go. Once you've determined that, as well as who is going and what it is you're going to do when you get there, you are now ready to plan for the vacation. This is where project management comes in. Project management is the vehicle that will help your organization in getting to its destination. The specific requirements for how project management becomes manifested in your organization depend very much on the needs of the organization.

To rely again on the example, if the destination of your family vacation is 4,000 miles away, then chances are the vehicle that will get you to your destination is an airplane. On the other hand, if the destination is only 200 miles from home, the likely mode of transportation is a car.

If you assume then that the appropriate mode of transportation for your family vacation is a car, there is still further planning to be done. You have to decide on the type, size, color, and make of that car. These variables will depend again on your family's needs. What I have observed in project management throughout my experience is that oftentimes people don't make the right choice of "car." Often the executives or managers who are tasked with adopting project management in their organization get wrapped up in "best practice," and they completely forget the whole exercise of "adapting" project management to meet their needs.

Most project management adoption exercises fail because the leaders in charge of this effort do not take into consideration that the standards for project management, such as those found in PMI's *PMBOK® Guide*, are simply a starting point for the discussion about what type of "car" you need. These standards offer the initial baseline for identifying the critical success factors. They are not a methodology to be adopted without tailoring. In fact, the power in these standards is the ability to select elements that take into consideration organizational context as well as factors impacting project management such as the organization's industry, region, functions, and so forth.

In his book *Who Says Elephants Can't Dance*, Louis Gerstner, the former CEO of IBM, said "truly great companies lay out strategies that are believable and executable. Good strategies are long on detail and short on vision." This is, indeed, where the power of project management comes in. In essence project management is about change. It is about enabling the organization and its leaders to navigate through the seas of change on efforts that involve building new products, offering new services, opening new markets, merging companies, or even downsizing. At its core, project management is not only a corporate tool, but a critical partner in implementing strategy. In effect, Lou's argument is that strategy that is not executable is not good enough. Executing strategy is the role of project management in the organization.

Effective project management in all its forms—managing a single project, a program (a series of related projects), and a portfolio (a group of projects and/or programs) – is a discipline that takes into consideration the needs of the organization and enables leaders to better manage transformation.

While there is significant benefit in the framework of processes and systematic approaches to project management, I want to emphasize the point that the benefit of project management to the small- and medium-sized organization is not the process and framework. It is the professionals and practitioners who are critical to successful delivery of the results of project management.

As we begin to explore the 10 principles of success in adopting project management into a smaller organization, it will become clear that leadership in project management is at the heart of achieving success. This is an important lesson because many organizations stress systems over people. Imagine an airline company hiring a bus driver to operate their Boeing 747 jet across the Atlantic. In essence, many organizations take actions similar to that. They want to implement effective project management using resources that are practically clueless on the needs and requirements as well as strategic fit of project management.

Culture and its role in the organization will be our starting point and the first principle of success.

KNOW YOUR CULTURE

"I came to see, in my time at IBM, that culture isn't just one aspect of the game – it is the game. In the end, an organization is nothing more than the collective capacity of its people to create value."

Louis Gerstner, former CEO of IBM,
Who Says Elephants Can't Dance

The Context of Culture

Shortly after I took up a new job assignment in Jordan in the spring of 2006, I participated in a prospective client visit to introduce the client to my company's project management consulting services. I remember sitting in the conference room with a colleague and a member of the client's team going over the importance of establishing a corporate project management office. The sales pitch felt more like a training session than an introduction to our services.

This prospective client was an ICT company and one of the more successful organizations in the region. They simply did not understand project management, but they were intrigued by the potential of implementing best practices in their organization.

In Jordan, this company is considered an enterprise-sized organization, but in the United Sates it would barely pass for a mid-sized organization. As we were going through the various topics, the CEO decided to drop in for a visit and learn for himself how project management could help.

The first thing that I did when he walked in was to stand up, smile, and extend my hand toward his to shake. As I began to speak my greeting in Arabic, he gave me a puzzled face, looked me straight in the eye and said: "Wow, I thought you were a foreigner. You smile too much for a Jordanian."

While I strongly believe that he had intended it as a compliment, I knew immediately that I had lost any opportunity in closing the deal. The CEO probably would never articulate it this way, and frankly neither could I at the time, however, but what I realized upon reflection was that a cultural barrier was immediately erected because of that subconscious action.

It's not that the CEO honestly believes that Jordanians don't smile. What he was really saying was that a Jordanian would not smile in the same manner that I did. He was able to sense from my adopted mannerisms that there was something different about me. That translated to a disadvantage, as I was unable convince him of the value that I bring as a consultant. He simply subconsciously assumed that I don't understand the culture.

And while regional/country culture is extremely critical in achieving success in business and on projects, there is another type of culture that is just as important. This is the organizational or corporate culture.

In the training workshops that we conduct, I ask the participants a rhetorical question: "Is there anything in the organization that is not affected by corporate culture?" Without fail, the participants either blurt out, or, after a short amount of reflection, say "No! Everything affects culture." Interestingly, however, I can state that without a doubt I have never been part of a project where we did not underestimate the importance of corporate culture.

The Power of Corporate Culture

Webster's dictionary defines corporate culture as "the set of shared attitudes, values, goals, and practices that characterizes an institution or organization." When I made my entry into IBM in 2000, I never truly appreciated what that meant. It's not that I had not been exposed to corporate politics of various degrees prior to the start of my career at IBM. On the contrary, my work as a project manager with a variety of organizations made me appreciate how important corporate politics were in terms of influencing project success. However, what IBM did was to fundamentally change my understanding of corporate culture. In fact, it expanded my appreciation for the fact that culture is not simply corporate politics, but rather it is the DNA of an organization.

From the moment that I started, I felt the power of corporate culture. I was flown into Raleigh North Carolina where I was enrolled into a two-day orientation program. This program was called "Becoming One Voice." The name in itself says volumes about IBM's belief in the importance of culture. It was a testament to the executive team's commitment to instilling IBM's culture within the new employees. It almost felt like a mixture of evangelism and brainwashing (in a good way, of course). The attitude that I had following this session was pure excitement and elation. I could not help but feel like I was part of a group of superheroes getting ready to conquer the world.

It was only after the conclusion of this program that my immediate manager was given "custody" of me. I flew to meet her and another colleague for the official assignment and hand-over of a project that was getting ready to be launched in a couple of weeks. I landed in LaGuardia Airport in New York and dashed over to one of IBM's offices in downtown Manhattan. The purpose of the meeting was to on-board me onto the project from the sales perspective so that I would be ready to conduct the kickoff meeting and meet the customer.

What first struck me about the whole experience was the sheer size of IBM. I often joke with people these days when they ask me about my IBM experience and say: "I worked for the small part of IBM. We only had 27,000 employees at the time!" It's true, as in the year 2000, IBM employed over 350,000 employees, most of who were working for its Global Services Division. Software Group, my division, was the smallest at the time. As you can see, everything is relative. Our division viewed itself as the small and agile part of the IBM enterprise, much like small- and medium-sized businesses.

The second thing that struck me was the level of organization and the systematic approach to project management. Here I was with my manager who happened to be a software developer by origin, and a colleague who happened to be from the business-development side of the house. Yet both individuals spoke the language of project management. IBM had instilled this language in its DNA. They did not specifically call it project management. However, every employee had to embrace the importance of execution, and that required at a minimum a fundamental understanding of project management. I later learned during my time at IBM that this language was common across divisions, countries, and continents. The power of IBM's culture was that it found its way into everyone's psyche.

The third observation was the speed at which this organization worked. Prior to joining IBM, I was working with a small consulting firm and I was outsourced on a client project. This client was what would be considered a mid-sized financial services firm in Des Moines, Iowa. The decision-making process that I had to jump through as an outsourced project manager between my own employer, the client organization, and other outsourced employees was hectic, to say the least. I was responsible for managing a multi-project effort in selecting and implementing a third-party software solution.

However, this responsibility did not come with actual authority to make decisions on behalf of the client. As such, I had to learn to create the appropriate conditions to allow the client executives to make decisions. That was not easy and did not happen quickly. It did condition me to become more patient to allow the various stakeholders to provide what was deemed as appropriate input before moving forward in a given direction.

So here I was, brand new to IBM but with my old mentality for decision-making based on this most recent experience. I remember in this initial meeting with my manager and colleague going over the proposed statement of work between IBM and the client. The statement of work (SOW) is a document that lays out the specific scope of activities that IBM planned to deliver to the client as well as the roles and responsibilities of both parties. In effect, the SOW provided the detailed parameters of the relationship between the parties.

As we were going through this document in preparation for its eventual signing by the customer and IBM, I provided what I considered several valuable points of feedback. At one point in the discussion, I started to get the feeling that there was so much that needed to be changed that we simply could not do it right then and there. So I made the suggestion to my manager that perhaps I should take the document overnight, make the appropriate changes, and come back to her and our other colleague in the morning with the updates. She gave my suggestion one second of consideration and immediately came back with the reply: "There's no time like the present. Let's make the changes now and together so that we don't waste another 24 hours of deliberations." Luckily for me, the suggestion that was shot down was not held against me.

I simply had to learn, and very quickly, that what was the norm in one organization a few weeks prior to joining IBM was no longer acceptable in my new circumstance. It's not that what I suggested was wrong—it's that it was wrong in my new context, the culture of IBM.

The most valuable lesson that I learned that day was that while it was nice to sit through two days of training to hear about IBM's culture, that was nothing in comparison to the on the job training of being immersed in the culture of my new organization.

What Works and What Doesn't

Another important element to success in project management that I discovered is the need to quickly figure out what works for a given organization and what does not. Several years ago I was hired by a regional consulting company to run a corporate project management office (PMO). The focus of my activities was on building a framework for managing consulting engagements as well as putting in place mechanisms for enhanced monitoring and tracking of project activities across the organization.

Based on some wise advice, the first step I did was to conduct an informal assessment of project management practices to determine what was then in place to support such an effort. I started the process by talking to various senior staff members to learn about the approach that was adopted for the projects. I also made sure to talk to key personnel outside of the senior staff. What I discovered was both interesting and disturbing at the same time.

While this organization did not have a standardized framework, methodology, process, or templates for approaching internal projects, the consulting team had developed a toolkit that was intended to be sold to consulting clients. This toolkit was called "PMO in a box."

The ironic thing was that there was a certain assumption in the consulting team that creating and/or implementing a PMO at a client organization was very much like installing Microsoft Office on a few laptops within a company. The assumption that they had was that all that was needed was a set of templates, a high level process, and a few walk-through sessions with client team members and—viola! Problem solved.

This thinking is fundamentally flawed. These individuals exhibited a lack of understanding of the fact that in addition to regional culture, corporate culture plays a significant role in adopting processes such as those in project management. Also, just as importantly, another element of culture that was completely discounted is industry culture. I have observed that while best practices in project management are generally applicable from one industry to another, a solid understanding of a given industry is imperative in tailoring the project management processes.

Let me explain how. Within this "PMO in a Box" toolkit there was a document that was called "requirements-gathering template." On first glance, it seems fairly logical and indeed prudent for a PMO to have such a document within its document library. However, when I inspected this template, I realized that it was specifically developed for use on software projects. So, following this logic, if the consulting team were to be hired by a client to build a PMO for a software development company or department, this template would come in extremely handy. However, what I learned shortly after I found out about this tool-kit was the fact that it was not only used on such clients, but also applied to other clients regardless of industry.

Now if you're dealing with experienced project management professionals, they will often have enough experience and know-how to start with such a document as an initial baseline then tailor it for the specific client needs. However, in this specific instance, the inexperienced project manager deployed this tool to clients outside of the software development industry with projects unrelated to information technology. The end result was a very frustrated customer and an unhappy project management team.

Following my assessment of the situation, I recommended that this "PMO in a Box" idea be shelved and a new framework be developed to address both agility and scalability in rolling out a framework that made sense in client situations. Furthermore, I engaged the project management professionals inside the organization to begin working together on developing an internal process for planning, managing, and tracking projects.

Interestingly enough, I also did not take into account corporate culture, as I ended up alienating several key stakeholders in the process. I first alienated the consulting team who worked on developing the idea for this toolkit. My feedback was perceived as a negative reaction to hard work and a job well done. It did not matter that I had a greater level of experience and understanding of project management. Their issue was not simply one of turf, although I am sure part of it was that. The issue at the core was that the team did not feel appreciated and my feedback was reinforcing a management misalignment to frontline resources working with clients.

In addition to alienating the consulting team, I also managed to alienate the senior executives in the organization. Attempting to highlight the fact that there had been project management processes implemented in the company prior to my arrival and without their knowledge exposed a lack of communication among these senior team members. It further highlighted the lack of coordination up and down the management chain. As such, my feedback was not well received. This made the job that I had to do all the more difficult to accomplish.

I was in an awkward position. Had I completely ignored the framework that was in place prior to my arrival, I would have still alienated the consulting team but perhaps kept the senior management team happy. On the other hand, if I had worked with the consulting team to issue a revision of this toolkit with elements that take into consideration customer needs diversity, the consulting team might have been more accepting. However, the senior management team would have likely been unhappy as they would have seen me signing off on what they considered to be mediocrity. I knew this to be the case as the CEO had told me often during this time that he brought me in to clean house, not maintain the status quo.

The lessons learned from this experience were indeed many and have helped shape greater appreciation in me for the need to embrace corporate culture as a foundational element in implementing project management best practices. The sad part, however, is that these lessons could never have been used in this role and with this organization. Sometimes the price for errors such as these is too high.

After navigating through corporate political hot waters, I came to another realization. Another important element of corporate culture is personal compatibility with it. Sometimes personal values, experiences, and skill-sets may be very much at odds with those of a given company. The individuals tasked with carrying out the implementation of project management best practices within an organization must be leaders who fully understand and appreciate the corporate culture of the organization. If they fail to understand and appreciate the culture, they are unlikely to be successful in implementing project systems and managing projects.

In many instances dealing with processes, tools, templates, and software specific to project management, I have seen leaders forget that the most important variable in the mix, the people. People are what makes up the corporate culture and without a healthy dose of respect for this, the leaders tasked with adopting or tailoring those best practices will likely fail.

People and Culture

It is easy to see that in organizations that are large, systems, legacy, and processes often drive and shape culture. However, in my experience, these play a lesser role in shaping the culture of a small- and medium-sized organization. Shortly before I joined IBM, I worked for a consulting company that had less than 50 people. Of these individuals 10 were considered management, 10 support staff, and 30 spread across various client projects. In this company, we discovered that setting a corporate culture for those individuals who were stationed on client sites was all but impossible.

What was puzzling to our management team was actually quite logical. The resources stationed at client sites actually ended up taking on the culture of their client. Indeed, I found myself adapting to the client culture and playing their corporate politics game.

It was actually a bit ironic at the time that upon joining this small consulting organization, I was handed a code of conduct manual that intended to encapsulate the corporate culture. Within this code of conduct document, there was a wide range of commands ranging from requirements for communicating to the home office to actual specifications outlining the need to shower regularly (at least once a day). My wife and I often joked about a certain phrase in the manual that actually encouraged employees to wear cologne.

Another small organization that I worked with had a similar employee manual that outlined what they called "the company way." Those of us who came from companies like IBM recognized the intention of this document. I later discovered that one of the senior staff members at this small company had been a former employee of a big-five consulting firm. He had let the HR manager borrow the employee manual from his previous job. The HR manager then conducted an advanced operation of copy and paste. This person had taken all the points from the big-five company and copied it into the small company's manual. The name was even similar. The result was, at best, laughable.

Within this manual there were several core values that did not make sense for this small consulting company. In fact, they only made sense if you applied them to the company that they were originally developed for. They included such things as commitment to customer situations, thought leadership, and ethical behavior. Not that these values are not good—what was missed was discussions, deliberations, and adoption by the small consulting firm. They weren't even valued by the senior management team. As a result, the resources working for this firm did not internalize them or live by them.

Another important element is the influence of individual leaders in small- and medium-sized organizations. I have previously mentioned the influence of CEOs like Lou Gerstner at IBM.

Imagine how much greater that influence is in a small organization where everyone knows everybody and each employee has the chance to interact directly with the CEO.

In the small consulting organization that I just highlighted, we had a CEO whose personality was larger than life. This person knew exactly how to influence people. Sadly, the influence took on the shape of manipulation as opposed to positive reinforcement. I personally witnessed many occasions where junior employees presented deliverables to this individual only to find themselves yelled at and accused of being incompetent and lazy. Can you imagine what type of reaction and behavior this ultimately resulted in? At a minimum, this accusation ended up being a self-fulfilling prophecy. However, often these tactics led to back stabbing and accusations.

This CEO was such a dominant personality that he inserted himself into most initiatives within the organization. His general thinking was that his presence would incentivize the employees to be on their best behavior and help raise the level of motivation. This type of involvement often back-fired resulting in the failure of the initiative and another round of finger-pointing and back stabbing. He also invited his senior team to meetings, tasked a specific individual with leading a project on behalf of the organization, then left the meeting and tasked a second person to work on the same initiative. His general belief was that this fostered a healthy level of competition. His theory was that if two people are working on the same thing, it showed the organization how important the effort was. He assumed that this again challenged people to do their best, assuming that the first to the finish would be rewarded. However, what happened more times than not, was a screaming match between the individual who finished the project first, the CEO, and the other individual. Everyone was accused of being incompetent and the project ultimately was closed out without delivering benefit to the organization.

Destructive leadership is one of the most difficult challenges that any organization has to overcome. Indeed, those of us who have found ourselves caught in such circumstances often found it easier to leave than to change the organization.

Structural Difficulties

Another very important factor that is both impacted by culture and affects culture is organization structure. A colleague of mine used to say that when it comes to change, one must start with people, then deal with process, and finally address structure. While I agree with this philosophy, I have come across many situations in my career where structure became an immovable barrier in the way of projects.

Project management experts may advocate that if an organization is interested in adopting good project management practice, there is a need to either completely overhaul an organization's structure or at least alter it in such a way to provide some sort of power and authority to the project management professionals. While I won't argue with this approach, what I have found is that the battle sometimes is so great and so exhausting that it may not be worth the fight.

At the onset of my career I worked for a college bookstore management company out of Chicago. This organization possessed a competitive advantage in its supply-chain management of books. It actually treated book distribution as if it were a just-in-time process for managing inventory by a company like Wal-Mart. Part of this company's success in this process was the set-up of corporate departments at the headquarters in support of their stores. These included departments like book distribution, store accounting, sales support, and merchandizing.

This company was structured along functional lines. In other words, the company was composed of various functional departments that execute the work. Each of these departments specialized in a specific function and provides those services to the rest of the company. So, for merchandizing, each a store would work with the merchandizing department to make their annual plans. Clearly, you would not call the accounting department to conduct this activity, as this would be outside of their specialization.

If I were to reflect on this company's structure today and consider turning it into something else, I am confident that this would create internal issues of such a scale as to cause loss of market share and a revolution by staff members. In this specific instance, the structure and the culture of the organization was fused together so drastically that any attempt at separating them might have brought down the entire organization.

On the other hand, if you compare this functional structure with a relatively projectized organization like IBM or perhaps a construction company, you will discover that the opposite is true. In the functional organization, the role of a project manager is most likely nonexistent, and in some cases it does not extend beyond simple coordination of tasks across certain departments. They are seen as administrative "grunts." However, in companies that are projectized, you will find that the role of a project manager is not only very well defined, but also carries a lot of organizational power with it.

I had personally experienced several situations within IBM where the project manager actually fired employees from their team. While this may not have been career-ending for the project team member, his or her role within that project came to an end.

Obviously the two previous examples are the extremes, and most organizations are likely to fall in the middle between the functional and projectized. Most organizations who undertake both departmental work and project work tend to build an organizational structure based on a matrix. This structure allows for functions to thrive and provides recognition that there are certain activities that need to be carried on by personnel who are not tagged to one department. The structures of power and influence in such organizations often are determined by cultural parameters such as staff seniority, general authority, likability of department heads, and CEO interest level.

Changing Culture

Changing corporate culture is often like attempting to help an individual overcome an addiction. I have seen instances where destructive behavior acts as a fire-feeding agent that prevents anything from changing the status quo.

The sad reality is that implementation of project management principles and adoption of a project management framework will almost always require culture changes within the organization. They often will manifest themselves in requests to change certain processes and introduction of new tools and templates. However, the fight will gradually expand to encompass elements beyond simple tools and procedures.

Changes to culture require that the senior leadership team in an organization, especially those in a small- and medium-sized company, not only be "okay" with the idea, but act as a full time champion and advocate on behalf of that change. Without this commitment, little is likely to happen to the organization and, as such, it won't take place. However, those tasked with implementing project management also have a job in support of the executives. They have to help them identity small and quick wins to better enable change. We will discuss this more in later chapters.

2

GET YOUR MIND STRAIGHT

"Move out of your comfort zone. You can only grow if you are willing to feel awkward and uncomfortable when you try something new."

Brian Tracy, Author on Leadership and Strategy

Over the past three years, our company has been working with a mid-sized company on strategy and transformation activities. We've had the privilege to be involved with this client pretty much from the beginning of the change effort.

We started the consulting engagement with an organizational strategy to better understand the organization, and then we facilitated the development of a strategic plan to chart a path for the future. Following the finalization of the high-level strategic planning process, we facilitated the executive team in identifying the specific measures of organizational success.

Using the balanced scorecard process, we worked with them to define goals, objectives, measures, and targets that are aligned with the vision, mission, and values of the organization. We were also lucky enough to support the identification of transformation initiatives or projects that the client organization needed to undertake in support of the strategy.

Once this process was concluded, our role transitioned from direct involvement to mentoring and coaching. However, we still had the opportunity to observe progress on the change effort. A couple of months ago we were facilitating a quarterly executive retreat to reflect on past progress and discuss what the team needed to do to continue the good work.

An interesting point came up during the discussion. While it was obvious that initially the progress in implementing the strategy was very slow, it seems that the last six months prior to the discussion proved to be extremely successful. As it turned out, much was accomplished in the way of initiating activities and transforming the organization.

That realization led to a discussion regarding execution in the organization. We were trying to understand why it was that projects in some cases were moving rapidly while in others were slow. The answer did not particularly relate to how well the organization had adopted or not adopted project management practices.

In fact, this company does not have a PMO, and for that matter does not have the critical mass in project management resources to consider itself capable of handling the change all at once.

The simple realization that we came to was that the organization had begun to see a change in behavior related to change and transformation. This change started first at the executive level and slowly began to trickle down to the other management levels. The behaviors and attitudes of the corporate leaders over the past six months had become more focused on delivering on the strategy, and as a result we started seeing greater movement on that front.

However, it was not as though they had not bought into the strategy previously. The issue was that the executives had not done anything to adjust their own behavior or that of their teams to support that strategy. It seemed that, in principle, they were bought into and excited about the strategy. In practice, however, very little action had taken place.

The difference over the six-month time frame was that each of the executives had taken it upon himself to work on furthering the strategy, and this type of behavior began to encourage other managers in the organization to do more in this vein.

As I reflect on the results of this engagement and the findings from this live case study, I realized that when it comes to managing change efforts (i.e. projects) there is something as important as understanding corporate culture, mastering the basics, having the right tools, and defining requirements. I discovered that attitudes and behaviors, both organizationally and individually, have a huge role to play in positioning the organization to either support or fight against that change.

The implementation of project management principles within an organization depends on a different mindset with a divergent set of behaviors to those present in purely functional organizations. That new behavior is tied to the psyche of the organization and impacts everything from corporate culture to organizational norms.

In the first chapter of this book, my focus was on trying to help the project management practitioner learn about organizational dynamics to appreciate what might work in an organization and what might not. However, in this chapter, I will address areas that I believe that the project management practitioners must focus on so that they are changed or altered to allow for greater effectiveness on projects.

While it is easy to recognize that organizational behavior is based on the culture of the organization, I believe that one must also appreciate that by changing behavior, the culture of the organization can change as well.

It's the Little Things

In his book *The Tipping Point*, Malcolm Gladwell discusses the importance of small things that have an impact on the larger picture. In one chapter, he talks about the crime epidemic in New York and what was required to take control of it and transform the city into a much safer environment.

In one example he cites, he talks about the city officials combating petty crime so as to impact major crime. One such effort was when the city workers on the subway made an effort to combat graffiti on subway engines and cars. He said that city officials believed that if the general public saw the subway in disrepair, there would be a greater chance of crime.

Another example that he gave is the "broken window" issue. He said that in neighborhoods where broken windows had gone unrepaired, there was a higher chance of crime because the criminals made the assumption that nobody really cared if a crime was committed.

The point that I am trying to make here is that when it comes to project management in small- and medium-sized businesses, sometimes it is the little things that make more difference than the large dramatic and sweeping changes.

I suspect that one reason for this is those who are committed to resisting the change tend to either ignore small changes or not see them all together. The big planned changes are easier to spot before they arrive and the resisters are much more likely to plan sabotage for their arrival.

There is definitely redeeming value to trying to implement small behavioral changes and affect certain attitudes to help the organization better embrace project management.

Consider for a moment the organization out there that never starts meetings on time. Perhaps this is a company where the executives are extremely busy and the CEO has to jump from one meeting to another. While management may not mean anything by starting late, the employees are sent the signal that either their meeting is unimportant or their project is not that critical. This type of behavior cascades throughout the organization to the point that every meeting is late and everyone contributes to the general waste of time.

It may be, in fact, that this small behavior is contributing to a general attitude in the organization toward project managers. Meetings called by project managers are seen as a waste of time because they start late or people don't show up to them because they have too many meetings to go to.

Imagine, for example, that the company has a brand-new CEO. He shows up to his first meeting on time, with an agenda, and ends on time. When another executive shows up late to the meeting, he is gently requested to show up on time. Imagine also that this meeting becomes a turning point for meetings in the organization where everyone starts to show up on time and the meeting leader is able to kickoff on time.

Suddenly this minor change in behavior has huge consequences in the organization. It may even begin to have an impact on the view of project managers within the company.

Decision-Making

Another element that has an impact on culture is decision-making. Obviously, decision making is impacted by behavior and the reverse is also true. The way that an organization makes decisions will often dictate how people interact with each other and how they accomplish tasks.

If you work for a company where team interviews happen before hiring a new employee, then that likely means that management values harmony or, on the flip side, everyone is afraid of taking decisions individually.

Having first established an understanding of the corporate culture, the project management practitioner should be fairly familiar with how decisions in the company are made. The next step in the maturity, though, is to explore the bad aspects of this process and identify ways for improving it.

During our work and observation of one client and their business environment, we noticed a very peculiar path to decision-making and issue resolution. For instance, we found that whenever there was a disagreement on a specific task in the organization, like how vacation time is calculated, the first thing that happens is that lower-level staff "agree to disagree." They then escalate the issue to their direct managers, which in this case are the finance and HR managers. These managers also never seemed to agree, so they escalated it to their managers, who were the vice presidents of the respective areas. Unfortunately, the vice presidents also were not able to come to conclusion, so they escalated it to the CEO for a decision.

The challenge is that by the time the disagreement came to the CEO's attention, it was four weeks too late. It then sat on the CEO's desk for another four weeks because of other pressing priorities and issues. By the time that the CEO had a chance to look at it, the issue either was resolved on its own or had mushroomed so that it was too large for anyone to resolve.

This example highlights a fairly typical way of dealing with issues and decisions with this client. As we began to explore why this was happening we received several points of feedback ranging from the employees feeling like they had no empowerment to the management feeling like the employees were not stepping up to do the job and make the tough decisions. I suspect that there was probably some truth to all the stories we heard. It may indeed have been the case that management had previously undermined employee decisions or the employees did not take accountability on issues and covered up for their actions.

The point is that the behavior was finally recognized, and discussed, and the client executives felt like they needed to do something to address the issue. Often, recognition is half way to resolution.

Execution and Decision Making

Previously I covered the linkage between organizational norms and execution. When it comes to managing projects, there has to be recognition in the organization that business-as-usual is not possible. The decision to adopt project management practices is usually based on a business case that can help justify changes to processes and decision-making systems.

It is up to the project management practitioners and those individuals responsible for adopting project management to ensure that there is an environment in the organization that is friendly to the practice of project management.

Behaviors and the Project Management Mindset

I have mentioned before that project managers are wired differently. Their mindset and that of project management in general does not work in the same manner as the rest of those in the organization. Having explored this point, let me outline some important behaviors that the project management practitioners need to champion to allow for better adoption of project management practice in their respective organizations.

- Work to defuse hallway discussions and post-meeting "meetings" and bring the dialogue back to the conference room table. This is especially important for organizations where the rumor mill is strong.
- Communicate both positive impact and negative impact of changes to the organization in a timely manner.
- Emphasize honesty to all project managers, even if they have to communicate bad news to executives. It's not that project managers are dishonest, but they sometimes have to temper their excitement and be a bit more realistic at their chances of side-stepping certain realized risks.
- Ensure that the project management practitioners are not isolating themselves from the rest of the organization, but rather are mingling with the project team members and functional staff.
- Ask lots of questions to ensure that everyone understands the end point and the vision of the project
- Keep your executive sponsors close and maintain constant connections to them, not just to ensure their support, but also to demand their attention, if need be.
- Say no to tasks that seem too big or battles that cannot be won. There is no shame in walking away to fight another day.
- Do not underestimate low-level employees and their influence on organizational norms.

- Build a support system within the organization for project managers so that they can feel like they are not the only ones facing challenges.
- Maintain a sense of humor in all that you do on these projects, as it will never cease to amaze you when humor is needed.
- Be flexible enough to ignore certain best practices if pragmatism can win more converts.

Perhaps the most important thing to remember when it comes to behavior and attitudes is that there is such a thing as being too idealistic. One has to remember that project management is a means to an end rather than a set of hard and fast rules that must not be deviated from.

3

CHAMPION THE VISION

"Obstacles are those frightful things you see
when you take your eyes off the goal."

Henry Ford, Founder of Ford Motor Company

I knew a classmate in college who must have changed majors at least four times. This was an individual who was not clear on what he wanted in life, he had no clue what he wanted to be when he grew up, and did not understand what strengths he possessed. Fortunately for him, we went to a liberal arts college that was a bit more helpful in supporting students like him.

The marketplace is not as forgiving as my four-year liberal arts college. If a company does not have a clear understanding of "what it wants to be when it grows up," it is likely going to end up nowhere. I saw this particular situation first-hand in one small-sized company. There was no definition of a vision for the organization, and as a result they lacked a plan to move forward. As a result, the company lacked the needed focus for success.

This was especially difficult on the sales and delivery teams. The sales team did not know which opportunities to go after to help further the organization's goals and the delivery team did not understand what constituted success in the mind of management. The result was a frustrating exercise in futility.

Unfortunately, I have noticed in my 20-year career that organizations in the small- and medium-sized space often lack a clearly articulated and unique strategy. Often I see vision statements along the lines of "we want to be the premier provider of services to our clients so that they are happy and allow us to grow." The problem with this type of vision is that it offers nothing to any of the company's stakeholders in terms of focusing them on enabling the company to achieve success.

As a result, project management professionals who are making an entry into a small- or medium-sized organization often find themselves in circumstances that require them to begin at the strategic level prior to considering the implementation of project management principles, defining best practices, or charting career paths for the project managers. Sadly, though, very few project management professionals have the skill-set, training, or experience in these situations that would enable them to truly impact the organization's strategic planning challenges.

Challenges in Setting Strategy

One of the most important activities that executives engage in while attempting to deploy project management to the organization is assisting the organization in defining and refining its strategy. In a small company, it is likely that these executives will have to do that on their own, without the input of external consultants, and with significant resistance from functional managers.

In order to successfully navigate this field of barriers, executives must become familiar with the potential challenges, which include:

- **Budgeting versus Strategic Planning.** I have often asked managers in small- and medium-sized organizations for their strategic plan. They have just as often produced a copy of their annual plan or budget. While having an annual budget is an important element of success tactically, having a strategic plan is a totally different proposition. The budget only provides a limited-time horizon in the life of a company and a limited field of focus—finance.
- **Alignment.** A 2006 McKinsey study found that 28% of companies that produce a strategic plan find its implementation ineffective, despite the fact that it reflects their goals and challenges. The same study found that 14% of companies produce strategic plans that are not aligned with their operations. I can imagine being part of the delivery team in such an organization. How can the individuals in operations succeed if the strategic direction does not take into account realities in delivery?

- **Planning Processes.** One challenge in small- and medium-sized organization is the lack of any formal (or even informal) processes related to turning the strategic plan into an actionable one. The result is, with no one taking accountability for making it happen, there is significant confusion as to what steps are necessary to implement.
- **Skill-Set.** Due to the limited bandwidth of resources, small- and medium-sized organizations often find themselves having to assign tasks such as strategic planning to individuals who are ill-equipped for the undertaking.
- **Communications.** Often either the wrong stakeholders are engaged in strategy—setting or the right stakeholders are not communicated with effectively. As such, little or no buy-in to the process's result is achieved.

I have found that being able to understand the above-mentioned challenges in strategic planning is a major contributor to overcoming roadblocks. However, to be clear, strategic planning is not an individual sport and, as such, another variable that affects success is the actual makeup of the team charged with setting strategy. While the project management professionals may step into an organization that lacks a formalized strategy, it is not realistic to expect that they alone can define the strategy of the organization.

The Process

Clearly, setting strategy is a process that requires a clearly defined lifecycle. In this manner, setting strategy is very similar to project management, as it also requires a lifecycle to establish an effective baseline for consistency. The process will obviously differ from one organization to another to account for cultural differences, industry requirements, and marketplace dynamics. However, the players will often be the same. These players include the following groups:

- **The Facilitator.** This person or team is responsible for leading the strategic planning exercise within the organization. While in large or enterprise organizations this role might be a senior executive, a consulting firm, or even a strategic planning department, in small- and medium-sized organizations this role could be assigned to anyone due to the nature of bandwidth constraints.
- **The Participants.** These individuals are the direct contributors to the content of the strategy. These include board of directors members, key executives and managers, and, in some cases, key external stakeholders.
- **The Contributors.** These individuals are groups who may be asked for specific feedback or input due to the nature of their relationship with the organization. It may be that they belong to a supplier group or a customer group with significant influence on the organization.
- **The Impacted.** These individuals are typically groups who may be affected by the strategy outcomes or may be directly tasked with implementing certain aspects of the strategy, such as a project team.

Project professionals along with key executives responsible for the adoption of project management standards in the organization have to be able to understand the dynamics taking place within these different stakeholder groups. Each group could very well have a different set of requirements and needs from the strategy, and, as such, may be pulling the organization in different directions.

It is very critical for the project professionals to champion the concept of organization project management as defined in PMI's *Organizational Project Management Maturity Model (OPM3®)*, which states that "organizational project management is the systematic management of projects, programs, and portfolios in alignment with the achievement of strategic goals." In a nutshell, project management is the connection between strategy and implementation within the organization. It is the enabling process that allows the organization to achieve its vision and strategic goals.

Indeed, project management application within organizations ranges from implementing strategy to product development. Projects may focus on delivering products and services or managing mergers and acquisitions. However, in every aspect of such activities, the most important element is to understand the context of project within the organization's strategy.

Executives and team members working on adopting project management principles or institionalizing its use must establish a clear understanding of the organization's strategic direction so as to create a strong link between the objectives of projects and the vision of where the organization is headed. This is particularly difficult in situations where project professionals are either not involved in setting strategy or, worse, are unaware of how strategy is designed within their organization.

Strategic Clarity

In 2006, I was leading an effort to assist an organization in a post-merger integration effort. As part of this scope of activity, our company was bringing together diverse teams and a variety of offerings within consulting and information systems. One challenge that seemed too great to overcome was an inability to reconcile organizational competencies. In other words, even though each company had a general definition of products and services, the new integrated company did not establish a clear direction for the integrated set of offerings.

The product teams came together to go over the details of each of the offerings and while a solid understanding was established for each of these offerings alone, there was no common vision for how the offerings would be packaged in the new company. Many discussions arose as to whether products should be aligned along industry lines versus functional specification. Other discussions seemed to lead the teams in diverse discussions on how to attack geographic markets.

It became apparent after several weeks of debate that the product teams and the delivery teams were not able to decide on the structure of the go-to-market approach and the delivery model. After some reflection, I began to understand that the challenge in this was primarily due to the fact that there was no cohesive vision for the new organization. The company did not have a defined strategic agenda. This lack prohibited the teams from coming together to develop a joint plan of attack.

While it was obvious the company possessed certain skills and talent, as well as a solid product offering in the marketplace, the fact that the strategy was blurry at best meant that this stumbling block was too significant to overcome. In the end, the teams found it difficult to form a common charter in presenting themselves to customers, suppliers, employees, and even competitors.

Saying No

Perhaps the greatest challenge shown from the previous example, and also seen in many other companies, is the executive team's inability, due to a lack of strategic vision, to turn down certain opportunities. Consider for a moment a consulting company that focuses purely on process reengineering. If the strategic direction for this company is to become a dominant presence in this market space in Europe, that means that when an opportunity comes along outside this scope, logic dictates it be turned down. However, I saw an instance when a company had an opportunity in North Africa for an employee salary-scale development project. Rather than turn down such an opportunity due to a lack of strategic fit, the company took it on.

Often, however, the executive team will find itself in a position of accepting the engagement because of financial considerations alone. As such, the delivery team is overburdened and faces bandwidth issues when the right opportunities present themselves. Furthermore, the company will often find itself dealing with major customer satisfaction issues as the project is outside of its realm of expertise.

Communication is King

Another area that requires focus in project management is communications. I remember attending a leadership conference a few years ago where one of the sessions was focused on strategy. During his presentation, the notable professor and author Michael Porter made the case that all stakeholders must know the company's strategy, even competitors. The challenge, however, is that often companies are afraid of making their strategies known, and in the process, forget to communicate to key stakeholder groups.

In one organizational assessment engagement that I took on in 2007, I interviewed the leaders of a customer organization. During these interviews, I asked the top 12 individuals in this client company to articulate the strategic vision. Not surprisingly, the CEO did a brilliant job describing where he saw the company going in the next 10 years. However, what I found extremely surprising was the fact that not a single other executive in the company was able to share a single element of this strategy. These other 11 individuals were not able to describe even the vision of the company, let along any financial goals and specific targets they were hoping to achieve.

Ironically, the CEO of the client organization assumed that because these executives were on the front lines and were in constant touch with each other, they immediately knew what the organization's strategy was.

Where is it Written?

In 2009, our company held a one-day executive forum. During the panel discussions, an executive in a premier organization made the case that strategic planning processes were a thing of the past. He stated that his company did not even have something called a "strategic plan." He also mentioned, however, that everyone in the company knew what the organization's strategy was.

The problem with this line of thinking is simple. How does one know what is expected of him or her as an executive and a manager if there is nothing that describes it in writing. A thought that is not written down is a thought that is likely going to be forgotten in today's marketplace.

Pipedreams and Realities

Perhaps the most important element in strategy-setting is the ability to implement it. If a strategy is simply an idea that is too difficult to implement, then it is a foolish strategy.

I remember being part of an organizational redesign in the late 1990s while being on the staff of a financial services organization. During that time, the organization engaged the services of IBM to help in the restructuring of the information systems division of the company. IBM sent us 10 highly experienced individuals with a significant amount of knowledge in the areas of restructuring and information technology.

The one area that the consulting team seemed to be lacking was knowledge of our organization. After spending over four weeks assessing the strengths of our company and identifying the weaknesses, the consulting team began an inventory process of all the information systems projects within the organization.

The consultants then held several strategic planning sessions with the information technology executives within our company. The end result was a detailed strategic plan that identified a vision for where the division was to go in support of the overall mission of the company. Alongside was a detailed IT governance plan and an IT architecture document that defined the needed systems, processes, policies, and projects needed for the overall transformation of the division.

Unfortunately, the document was missing an assessment of the available skill-set present in the organization to undertake this transformation. This significant element was completely ignored. The information technology division within our company at the time was heavily focused on mainframe software development and implementation. The mainframe development activities constituted primarily COBOL programming language skill-sets. This made sense because most of the systems within the organization were housed on the mainframe, including the company e-mail systems.

The new IT strategy, however, called for the implementation of emerging technologies such as Java based solutions. The problem lay in the fact that not a single computer programmer in the company was aware of or even had any knowledge of these programming languages.

The new strategy did not account for the fact that every single employee in the IT division had to either go back to training to retool, or the IT division had to fire all its employees and hire new ones. After significant exploration within the market, the consultants and the IT executives were told by the human resources department that the skill-set needed in the new structure was not even present in our state. That meant that the IT division had to worry about recruiting staff from major markets with salaries unrealistic for our state. The other option was to send everyone to training, which was also unrealistic.

The bottom line was that the strategy for this major division within this medium-sized financial services company could not be implemented. The plan was far removed from reality and, as such, had to be redefined to match the marketplace and facts on the ground.

Had such an issue been identified at the onset of the strategic planning cycle, the plan would have taken into account the need for developing a strategy that was implementable in the current conditions.

This example demonstrates how valuable the skill-set of project management, risk mitigation, and project planning is to such efforts as strategic planning. Being able to bridge the gap between strategy and delivery is what project management is all about. Having the ability to translate vision into reality using project management tools, while leveraging the skill-set between long terms planners and detailed implementation resources, is something that can be of extreme value to the organization.

Linking Project Management to Strategy

> *"The concept of organizational project management is based on the idea that there is a correlation between an organization's capabilities in project management, program management, and portfolio management, and its effectiveness in implementing strategy."*
>
> – PMI's *Organizational Project Management Maturity Model (OPM3®)*

As previously mentioned, there is a strong correlation between success in project management and the ability of project professionals to link their projects, programs, and/or portfolios to the strategy of the organization.

This process starts by having project management practitioners who understand the viewpoint and perspective of the executives of a given company or organization. Having this perspective means that the project management practitioners will become privy to the challenges faced by the executives and can begin to position themselves in situations that help the executives in resolving their challenges and problems.

On several occasions during dialogue with senior executives of organizations of varying sizes, I have had the opportunity to ask the following question:

If we were to assume that the conditions of achieving success in your organization include the following:

- Creating an innovative organization strategy
- Aligning day-to-day actions to long-term plans
- Building a professional corporate culture
- Fostering employee growth and loyalty
- Leveraging the power of leadership toward excellence

What is it that you need in order to achieve the above definition of success? The answer is usually something like this:

> *"We first have to be able to define a corporate vision that we can rally the organization around. Second, we have to align organizational performance to the corporate strategy. Third, we have to ensure that the organization has enough diversity in terms of skill-set to ensure that weaknesses are compensated for. Fourth, we have to meet financial bottom line results so as to keep the owners and stakeholders happy with the organization's performance."*

As one begins to form a mental picture of the above scenario, another perspective emerges regarding executives. This perspective is built on the fact that oftentimes project managers do not share the same set of worries that executives have in terms of leading their organization and teams. Here's a sampling of the comparison:

- Executives have to worry about meeting revenue and bottom line targets, while project management practitioners have to worry about cost baseline.
- Executives have to worry about creating value for the shareholders, while project managers have to worry about delivering their projects on time and within budget.
- Executives have to worry about satisfying customer needs to ensure repeat business, while project management practitioners worry about meeting product/service specifications.
- Executives worry about beating the competition, while project managers have to worry about the project baseline parameters.
- Executives worry about sustainability, while project managers worry about transformation and change.
- Executives worry about being relevant in the eyes of their employees and organizations, while project managers are focused on delivering the project and transitioning the project team.

It is not to say that one perspective is more important than the other; however, it is extremely important to understand that project management practitioners have to develop a bridge between their perspective and that of the executives. If the project, program, or portfolio manager is not able to alleviate the worries of the executives in achieving their baseline results, their effort is likely going to yield frustration as opposed to strategic success.

In small- and medium-sized organizations, the interaction between strategy and operations, vision and delivery, executives and project managers tends to be more frequent. The lines are blurred to a greater extent and expectations tend to be less defined.

Individuals tasked with ensuring success in adoption of project management standards and practices find themselves living these realities and have to adapt their practices to blend strategy and implementation to ensure continued organizational viability and success.

Helping executives juggle the competing needs of customers, suppliers, and employees in achieving the organizational strategy becomes a chief concern in this matter.

Internal Champions

Leaders who are responsible for implementing project management practices within small- and medium-sized organizations find themselves in the position of internal champions for project management. This, however, is not enough. These leaders must also take on the role of vision and strategy champions on the project, program, and portfolio side. They have to enable the project management practitioners to see the linkage between their projects and the organization's ultimate vision.

The ability to do so is predicated on being able to build a unique culture that blends strategy and execution and understands that project management can yield competitive advantage.

It is important to note that that success in this area begins with establishing the right level of buy-in for project management in the organization, which we will discuss further in Chapter 4.

4

ESTABLISH THE BUY-IN

"Am I not destroying my enemies when I
make friends of them?"

Abraham Lincoln, 16th President of the United States of America

Early in my career in project management, it seemed that the profession was not clearly understood and the value was not appreciated. In fact, I saw many examples of clients actually refusing to pay for consulting services associated with a project manager. It was almost an expectation that if a client was spending a certain amount of money on a project, they should receive the project management services for free.

This, in fact, was very similar to the way IBM did business prior to the 1980s. At the time, IBM sold hardware and there was an expectation that software and services would be given for free as part of the hardware purchase. It took IBM quite a while to realize that the resources expended on developing software should not be given for free, as there was a cost associated with them. IBM had to build buy-in with clients to make them appreciate this. Additionally, IBM had to do the exact same thing with services rendered in association with selling the hardware and software.

During my early days as a project manager, I found myself in the role of advocate on behalf of the profession simply so I could convince the client that my role on the project was needed. I have heard of similar experiences from colleagues.

Several years ago, an application development company for which a colleague was a project manager won a contract with the state government for implementing a new electronic application system. It seems that at the time of contract signing, the client refused to include the services associated with the project manager. So my colleague's manager wisely decided to change the title of the project manager to business analyst.

My colleague was initially a bit apprehensive and not sure how to best meet expectations. However, as time passed, the client began to understand the value of what this person was providing to the team. Slowly, their views began to change. In fact, when my colleague left this company to take on a different assignment with another employer, this client insisted that my colleague be replaced with another project manager because this person finally understood the value that this person brought to the team.

As a project manager in small- and medium-sized businesses, I have often found myself in similar situations where I had to advocate for the adoption of project management in an organization. I had little to do with organizational strategy or even the decision to adopt project management. I was typically brought into the organization because some other individual leader sold the idea to the CEO and the executive team. As such, I had to become familiar with the strategy, culture, and needs so that I could become an effective salesman on behalf of the profession.

Executive View of Project Management

A few years ago, PMI issued a survey to senior executives asking about their attitude toward project management and specifically the project manager. One question asked executives whether they believe that project managers in their organization are empowered to get the job done and have influence in the enterprise. The response by these executives was overwhelmingly yes. To those of us who have been in the role of project manager, we found the results of this survey puzzling. Most of us have seen firsthand situations where project managers at best were on the fringe of power and influence in organizations.

Wanting to understand this puzzling situation, PMI followed the survey with a focus group consisting of a sub segment of those surveyed to try and better understand the discrepancy between the executive view of the project manager and the project managers' view of their own situation. The focus group pointed out that what executives consider "project managers" is a totally different group from what project management practitioners consider as project managers. In this specific situation, executives assumed that project managers are leaders in their own organization who happened to have a senior executive role in a specific function (e.g., vice president of marketing), who also were tasked with "managing" a specific project on behalf of the CEO.

In reality, this individual who was tasked by the CEO to lead this given initiative is actually, in project management terminology, the sponsor of that project and not the project manager. However, what this survey pointed out was the fact that there was a significant gap in the executives' understanding of project management and the role of project manager.

Leaders tasked with rolling out project management practice in small- and medium-sized organizations will undoubtedly face a similar situation in trying to establish buy-in, as it often starts with explaining what project management really is.

I saw it several times in my career in designing, launching, managing, and transitioning PMOs. The terminology for such offices is not standardized and as a result each time I had to sit down with the leadership team to establish a common language as to what this PMO truly is. A good place to start was to understand what the executives were trying to accomplish and how many projects they envisioned this PMO overseeing.

Among the most common misconceptions that I've run into in trying to establish buy-in for project management include:

- Executives thinking that project management is an operational activity that is part of a delivery unit such as a manufacturing department
- An assumption that a project manager is a technical person such as an engineer or a computer programmer and not a business person
- A view that project management is simply a tool (like Microsoft Project), and not a framework of management

- A belief that anyone can be a good project manager if they were a good performer in their specific departmental functional role, such as engineering or sales

However, none of the above-mentioned items are nearly as dangerous as the tendency by some executives to either lump everything into projects or nothing at all. Organizations are usually a lot more complex than that. Typically, most companies will have both operational or functional processes and project activities. Consider the difference between managing daily accounting transactions as compared to the deployment of new accounting software. The first is an operational process, while the second is a project activity with a clear beginning and an end.

Selling project management to the organization or establishing buy-in for the framework of project management starts with understanding the need. This is a subject that I will cover in Chapter 9. However, it is equally important that organizational stakeholders develop a fundamental understanding of project management.

That does not mean the organization should enroll senior managers and team members in a Project Management Professional (PMP)® certification preparation workshop. On the contrary, project management understanding has to be specific to the function that each stakeholder group performs and the specific interaction with the projects within the organization. Training has to be tailored to the needs of the organization. It should take into account global best practices that need to be leveraged in assisting the organization to improve its delivery functions and linking its projects to the vision and mission of the company.

The goal of establishing buy-in is to convince the various stakeholders within the organization that the introduction or refinement of project management practice within the organization will improve the organization and make everyone's life better.

Ultimately, actual achievement will have a significant role in realizing the needed buy-in, and as a result, quick wins that demonstrate progress are strongly recommended.

Buy-in and Change Management

"It is not the strongest of the species that survive, nor the most intelligent, but the one most responsive to change"

—Charles Darwin

One of the very first assignments that I was involved in as I began my project management career was a third party software implementation project involving scanning and imaging technology. The focus was on reengineering processes in the membership and billing department at a healthcare insurance company. Interestingly enough, the company had been through a couple of iterations with different technologies prior to my joining. Both previous efforts resulted in frustration and ultimately the cancellation of the project.

Luckily for me, I was not tasked with managing the project but rather was allowed to "observe" as part of becoming better oriented with the organization. The kickoff meeting was held literally on the second day after my start date. I remember riding in the car with my manager, going to the off-site kickoff meeting. She had joked that the location was not a good omen for the success of the effort, as it was held in the warehouse facility rather than the corporate headquarters.

The project team consisted of managers in the areas affected by the implementation, IT resources, as well as some resources who would ultimately become users of the system. Initial discussion focused solely on defining functional requirements and gaining a better understanding of the requirements as related to the process. As the project started moving through the various phases of planning and implementation, we noticed more and more flags being raised by the user group. There was a significant amount of concern especially because several had assumed that once the system was fully implemented, their jobs would be made redundant and they would be fired from the company.

The problem was that there was no communication with the users about the plans for the department and its structure following the implementation. The executives did not even consider laying off any resources following the implementation. In fact, the executives had assumed that the software would allow the company to better handle the process and as a result would not have to hire additional resources in the membership and billing areas to handle growth. Unfortunately, however, this piece of information was never shared with the user groups. The team had operated on the principle that knowledge is power and the less they communicated, the better.

Shortly after the completion of the development and installation phases, the third-party implementation consultants conducted a one-day training session for the users and administrators. They finished deployment of the hardware and made a quick exit from the organization. In principle, the system seemed to be functioning very well and the data that was previously only available in hard copy was now available online and the images were saved in electronic format.

A few months after the system was fully operational, a sister department to our project management office that focused on quality improvement went back to the membership department to conduct a process audit. The aim of this exercise was to determine if the system implementation had yielded the benefit that was intended for the organization. Some of the measures they were looking for were things like increased employee productivity, speed of processing of membership applications, and accuracy in data entry. One data point that was critical was management's assumption that that with the introduction of this scanning technology, data entry errors would be significantly reduced, as there was less room for human error.

The process audit results were very surprising to the organization. The project team members were shocked and the management was furious. On most of the elements in the assessment, it was determined that the system implementation did not reduce the time for processing applications, it did not increase productivity, and data entry errors were not eliminated.

What added insult to injury was that the director in charge of membership and billing had submitted yet another request for management to increase the number of staff members assigned to processing membership applications by 17 additional data entry clerks to handle the increased volume of applications.

The results of the process exercise and the request for the additional staff got the attention of senior leaders in the company. The CEO sent an urgent note to one of the executive vice presidents asking him to personally look into the problem. I remember very vividly that the executive vice president did not simply call a meeting of the project team or of the senior leaders and sponsor of the project. He did something that I considered to be extremely wise at the time. He asked the project team along with the key senior leaders to meet him on the floor of the department where the scanning and imaging process took place. After spending 15 minutes observing the membership application processing team using the system, every single person on the project team was able to figure out for themselves why the project did not yield the intended positive results in the organization.

It turned out that while the new fancy system offered a lot of bells and whistles for the department team such as the introduction of large monitors, none were actually used as intended. Prior to the implementation of the system, data entry clerks used the physical handwritten membership application to enter data into the mainframe. The system introduction was expected to eliminate that by having the form scanned and data populating the mainframe directly from the new software. However, the data entry clerks were bypassing the new process. While they did scan the physical membership application form, rather than simply review the electronic data to make sure it was populating properly, they did not save it and opted to actually re-enter the data manually from the physical form. The bottom line was that the multi-million dollar implementation ended up being nothing but an expensive photocopying machine.

Fortunately, the team regrouped and worked together to try and enhance the process. Management had to ultimately divide the data entry clerks from the scanning process to not allow them even access to the hard copies. That was the only way the organization saw any positive results.

I often reflect back on this project as a very valuable lesson in managing expectations and establishing the needed buy-in on projects. The project team, who interestingly did not really have a clear project manager, forgot to involve the user group appropriately in the business-case development. The team did not communicate effectively with user groups to alleviate the concerns that the employees had regarding the system. In fact, the user group was all but ignored and their potential concerns all but forgotten. However, as the team discovered, buy-in from the user group caused significant challenges and made the team look bad in front of the entire organization.

This valuable lesson taught me that buy-in is perhaps the most important element that project management practitioners need to focus on ensuring that there are mechanisms to engage key stakeholder groups impacted by the project and gaining their support and buy-in. The same would also be true for project management practitioners responsible for deploying project management principles in the organization. Buy-in is a must, not a nice to have.

Stakeholder Influence

When it comes to buy-in, one important consideration is that project management is a discipline focused on change. Projects themselves are undertaken to affect change in the organization. Whether the objective of a specific initiative is to build a product, deliver a service, or transform a process, projects focus on creating a different future for a given organization or client. It is important in the process of achieving buy-in to acknowledge to the project stakeholders that the future will be different and the result will have an impact on these stakeholders. Buy-in starts with helping the impacted parties understand how their life or work will be different once the project is completed. Similarly, when implementing project management in an organization, stakeholders have to understand that the way they do work will be different.

The successful leaders will try and help stakeholders understand how life will be changed for the better, rather than for the worse. This is particularly critical, as human beings fear change. People don't like to operate in the realm of the unknown, and one way to help them navigate this process is stating that project managers are professionals who are trained to manage the unknown. An example of this process is highlighting how risk management can help improve chances of success due to the rigor of mitigation planning.

As part of this process, it is important to try and figure out what category a potential stakeholder might fit in when it comes to their support or lack thereof of projects and project management. I have typically categorized stakeholders into the following categories:

- **The Champions.** These are people who are totally bought into the concept and its intended benefits. They find themselves advocating for the change. The best way to manage the relationship with these people is to not waste time convincing them of the benefits of the change—after all, they are already won over.

- **The Supporters.** These are individuals who think the intended change is going to bring about a positive result. They are willing to support the change because they've made a leap of faith. It is important that these people feel like their feelings of support are justified. Their feedback should not be ignored and they should not be alienated.

- **The Indifferent.** These people don't care one way or the other when it comes to the intended change. They are not sure if they will benefit from the change, so they are passive about it and are not likely to take an active role in fighting it. They may sympathize with the objectives of a given project, but have not figured out how it will directly help them. It is important to try and shift these people into the camp of supporters or champions. This is best done by figuring out what these people care about and attempting to demonstrate that their needs will be met once the change is implemented.

- **The Antagonists.** These are individuals who are convinced that the change will bring about negative consequences for them and will fight against it. They will often attempt to discredit the team, the idea, and the leaders responsible for the change. While it might seem important to neutralize these threats, unfortunately energy spent on either attempting to convert these people or fighting them is wasted energy. It's important to be aware of their movements to sidestep potential traps. Ultimately, however, there is nothing better to neutralize these people than success.

Agents of Change

Another element to consider in achieving buy-in and managing change is to develop a greater understanding of the different roles involved in change, specifically implementing project management:

- **Project managers.** These are the leaders who are responsible for facilitating change in organizations. Project managers are change agents because they typically are wired differently from leaders who manage functions and processes within organizations.
- **Sponsors.** These leaders are executives who are responsible for achieving the desired result from the project. They are the customers of the projects within the organization. Their job is to provide support for the project managers and team members to help achieve buy-in on projects.
- **Project team members.** These are individuals tasked to work on projects. Their role in supporting the management of change is to help the organization be prepared for the change. A major role is explaining that the "evil that we know" is indeed worse than the "evil we don't know."
- **Key executives.** These are leaders in the organization that typically have institutional power and are able to directly influence the organization and other stakeholders. When it comes to adoption of project management practices within the organization, receiving buy-in from these executives is key.
- **Department heads.** These are individuals who will have a primary interaction point with individuals responsible for managing projects. They might initially provide a significant amount of resistance to project management because they could see the processes under their control changing and their domain of influence eroded.

External Stakeholders

Another group of people who might be impacted by change and indeed may require some level of buy-in are individuals outside the organization. I remember in the late 1990s, I interacted with IBM delivery teams as a customer. IBMers spent a significant amount of time trying to convince clients how important it was to assign project managers on projects. I recall situations where some of our executives within the client organization argued that the project does not need a project manager, as there was an entire team involved. IBM, on the other hand, was adamant about this and managed to convince our executives of this. The bottom line was that IBM at the time was willing to put their money where their mouth was. The IBM executive told our executive that they will assign a project manager and if we were not happy with his performance and contribution to the team, we should not worry about paying for his services. It worked.

Other external stakeholders that may need buy-in will likely include suppliers of the organization. This is especially true in situations where the organization feels like dictating terms to their suppliers. If the organization is powerful, like Wal-Mart, this buy-in takes the form of demands. However, in small- and medium-sized organizations, persuasion is likely the path forward as opposed to demands for adherence to organizational policies and practices.

Managing Expectations

Managing expectations is another significant input to achieving stakeholder buy-in. This process starts by attempting to set those expectations before the change process begins. Expectations can either be stated or unstated. In my career, I have noticed that the most successful project management practitioners are those individuals who are able to identify unstated expectations and negotiate with stakeholders in terms of setting these expectations.

In several of the workshops that I lead on change and implementing project management offices, I asked the participants to answer a simple question. I present them with a slide that has the following words:

Red (the workshop slide shows this word in blue)
Blue (the workshop slide shows this word in red)

Following this slide I ask the group, which of the above listed items is red and which one is blue. Obviously there is no right or wrong answer to this question. The point is that often times expectations stem from perception. If the change agent is able to influence the perception of those impacted by the change, the chances for buy-in improve tremendously. This process is helped also by proper documentation and communications, especially in trying to overcome negative perceptions.

Perspective

Small- and medium-sized organizations often face certain challenges that highlight the opportunity to implement the practice of project management. These challenges are typically a good starting point to address so as to achieve buy-in for the discipline. They include:

- A lack of understanding as to why a given project is undertaken and no clarity as to the need that justifies the expenditure
- No visibility or link between projects and the organization's objectives
- No consistent approach in planning and managing projects, causing a lack of consistency in delivering projects on time and under budget
- High levels of turnover in the staff assigned to work on projects or lead them
- Ambiguity in stakeholder expectations and lack of knowledgeable resources

Being able to identify the challenges or the "as-is" situation in the organization can be a helpful baseline to demonstrate that once the change in the organization is adopted, several of these challenges can be addressed. This could range from improved customer delivery and satisfaction, greater linkages with strategic objectives, improved executive interactions, greater clarity in expectations, and improved career development for project managers.

Buy-in and Communications

In order to achieve clarity on the objectives of the positive changes intended by the adoption of project management in the organization, the leaders responsible for this effort must develop clear messages to the various stakeholder groups. These messages have to be tailored by group to ensure proper understanding. The communications have to be clear enough to communicate adverse news honestly. Messages also have to be delivered in a timely manner so as to combat the "grapevine" effect within the company. It is important not to delay or put off issues that pop up in the rumor mill. Ultimately, communication is about alleviating the fear of change, thus achieving buy-in.

5

BUILD UNCONVENTIONAL LEADERSHIP

"Leaders are made, they are not born. They are made by hard effort, which is the price which all of us must pay to achieve any goal that is worthwhile."

Vince Lombardi, Legendary American Football Coach

A common theme that I have often seen in small- and medium-sized organizations is the fact that individuals often matter more than systems and processes. That is not to say that in a company like IBM where there are thousands of employees, management does not care about people—in fact, the opposite is true. What I mean, however, is that small- and medium-sized organizations often rely too much on individuals in various leadership positions, almost to the detriment of the organization.

What I discovered in these types of businesses is that due to the absence of institutionalized processes, certain individuals tend to hold information close to the vest. As such, they are likely to be in a position of power over the organization and the employees. This model is neither scalable nor sustainable. It actually fosters an element of firefighting in the organization. A colleague used a saying to describe I the trouble with a firefighting culture in companies. She said that firefighting breeds arsonists. My experience has taught me that this is nearly universally true. Whenever you have a culture that relies heavily on individuals as opposed to teams and processes, you experience hero complexes.

Imagine, for instance, a city that is overrun with crime. This is a city that might have problems with disease, theft, murder, drugs, and general violence. In the context of our culture today, we understand this city to have a high degree of lawlessness and we intuitively know that something needs to be done. Consider for a moment that most of us have seen movies such as Superman, Batman, and Spiderman. Now, I wonder how many rational adults would immediately suggest having "Superman" come in and clean house and fix the city's problems. Most rational adults know that Superman cannot do this because he is a figment of someone's imagination.

If we assume, however, that the city takes a miraculous turn for the better, the likely scenario is that the true superheroes are the police officers, the firefighters, the civil servants, and the ordinary people who worked together to help the city resolve its problems.

Now, let's go back to the hero complex in organizations. Why is it that with organizations, which are presumably run by rational adults, we find leaders who expect Superman or Batman to jump in and rescue them from their problems? Why is it that we see executives in such organizations fostering this behavior and rewarding it when it takes place?

The first thing that executives of small- and medium-sized organizations have got to recognize is that project management is a team sport where superheroes are not allowed. People matter, but there is no place for the individual.

Knowledge, Skills, and Experience

One of the first activities that I initiated shortly after I was appointed PMO director of a company in the Middle East was to begin assessing the level of talent present in the project managers in the organization. I was charged with "getting a handle" on the project managers to ensure enhanced performance. The company's CEO wanted me to elevate their skill-set and inspire them beyond their potential at the time.

While the company certainly had the superhero complex that I discussed earlier, a bigger problem was the lack of teamwork. Individuals in the organization refused to see that they were on the same side. In fact, they rejoiced when a colleague was in trouble or his or her project was plagued with issues.

One of the most bizarre aspects of people's attitudes was their view of their own ability and capability. In attempting to meet the tasks that was charted for me, I engaged each of the project managers in a dialogue about their performance, experience, and skill-set. I certainly did not feel at the time, at least immediately, that I could make a call on how to evaluate them. I invited them to complete a self assessment for the purpose of working with me on creating an individual development plan to enhance their ability to manage projects.

Since the budget that I had was extremely limited, I had to rely on previous experiences to shape a tool that I ended up developing to help with the exercise. Working with a couple of colleagues, we developed a list of 20 questions that attempted to address three areas:

- Knowledge
- Skills
- Experience

Each of the questions typically focused on one of the three areas with the ability to comment so that we could work later with the project managers to better understand their perspectives. The responses of these questions included a five-point scale that the individual selected for their self assessment.

A sample question could have been something like "In my project management experience, I have been involved in vendor management activities in accordance with chapter xyz of the *PMBOK® Guide.*" The individual then selected one of the below answers:

- 1 = "I have no knowledge of the subject"
- 2 = "I've read about it, but have no practical knowledge"
- 3 = "I can do it with limited guidance"
- 4 = "I can do it by myself"
- 5 = "I can do it and teach others how to do it"

Without fail, every single one of the 10 project managers reporting to me at the time selected either #4 or #5 on every single answer. Interestingly enough, I too spent time to conduct an assessment of my own skill to see how it would compare, and

I was shocked that my own self assessment was significantly lower than the self assessment of my project managers.

I had finally come to a harsh conclusion. In attempting to develop my people, I could not rely on them to help me "help them." This might have been attributed to a fear culture where they felt threatened in admitting points of weakness. The bottom line is that while developing people is important, the method of doing so in this time of small- and medium-sized companies has to be different from the traditional approach used at a company the size of IBM. In point of fact, I know that IBM uses a very similar tool that most of my colleagues have no problem in completing accurately to help advance their career.

Who is a Project Manager?

During PMI conferences around the globe, I often joked with colleagues that the project management profession would not advance to the degree that we needed it to until such time that our grandmothers would understand what a project manager does.

In fact, during most encounters in the 1990s I would often meet people in social gatherings, and, after short introductions, they would ask me what I did for a living. I would respond, "I am a project manager." They would then smile with a glazed look on their face. Those who were brave enough would follow up with "and what does that exactly mean?"

Later, in the early 2000s, the profession of project management was not helped when the Donald Trump television show called "The Apprentice" introduced the audience to the concept of the project manager. Sadly, in many instances these so-called project managers exhibited behaviors that I would have considered totally unprofessional or counterintuitive to project management.

It's the Leader, Stupid

One of the first points of advice that I provide to my consulting clients is that a project cannot exist without a project manager. Yet so many organizations, especially small- and medium-sized ones, seem so comfortable launching projects without people leading them.

Believe it or not, however, this is not the worst sin that an organization can commit in dealing with projects. Having an incompetent person in charge of a project can do a lot more harm than a project that is leaderless.

One perfect example that illustrates the incompetent project manager is a situation I encountered again as an observer of a project. I had been at the time a project manager assigned to a corporate PMO. The marketing department within the company had planned to launch a new product. Given the nature of the project and the importance to the marketing department, they refused to involve the PMO in the initiative. They decided instead to assign a project manager from the marketing department. This individual actually even carried the title project manager.

I was fortunate enough to attend his kickoff meeting where over 40 people from different departments were present. He showed up to the meeting 10 minutes late and after all the seats were taken. He opted to stand in the middle with his back pointed to at least half a dozen people. He came to the meeting without a notebook, even though he had nobody taking minutes for him. He did not have an agenda, there was no presentation, and there was no mention of a project charter. I found out that the people in the team came not because they were assigned to the team, but rather because he was a likable guy and he invited them thinking that they would join the team once they heard how great the project was.

Shortly after he said hello, he spent five minutes rambling on about the project and how it was a strategic one for the company.

The discussion was very shallow and did not address any specific points regarding its link to the strategy or even the scope involved in delivering it.

The highlight of the meeting came when a person in attendance asked the project manager a question related to legal issues associated with the product. The project manager then replied that he had gotten some department within the state government to provide an official answer to that very question. He then decided that it would be best to go back to his desk to get the letter and provide everyone in the room with a copy of it. One of his friends offered to go get it and make copies on his behalf. He was told that he would not know where to look. The project manager then proceeded to leave his "kickoff meeting" for over 15 minutes, leaving everyone with nothing but to time to discuss everything except the project.

Not surprisingly, that kickoff meeting was probably the best thing that happened to that project. It went downhill from there and finally ended much like a train wreck would end, miserably.

The bottom line is very simple. A project manager is like a bus driver. If the bus driver leaves his seat while the bus is moving, bad things will happen. The project manager must not only be in his or her seat at all times, but they have to also drive the bus.

Not all Project Managers are Created Equal

As stated previously, project managers are often wired differently from other employees and managers. So if leaders start with this assumption in mind, then they have to explore what it takes to interact effectively with project managers. They also have to consider how to structure the organization's relationship with these individuals to position them for success. There are several considerations that need to be looked at. They can be looked at using the following questions:

- Are there clear job descriptions for project managers providing a solid understanding of what they are supposed to focus on and how they are going to be evaluated?
- Does the company have established entry criteria so that individuals who are hiring project managers understand that there are experience requirements along with knowledge and skills? Are there requirements for certification?
- What is the right mix of industry knowledge and technical expertise needed to perform in the role of project manager adequately?
- Does the company have a defined career path for the project manager? Most project managers thrive on the challenge of managing change, not processes. As such, is there a career path that helps these individuals grow? What happens if they cannot grow—is the company okay with them leaving?
- Where is the best place to position these project managers in the organizational chart? Is it better to group them in one department such as a PMO or is it better to scatter them in various departments to allow for improved business links?
- What ways will the company establish to differentiate the project managers based on contribution and performance within the organization?
- Who is best suited to manage these project managers, a functional manager or someone with experience managing projects?
- How should these project managers be compensated in relation to the company standards and industry requirements?

I have often asked individuals in my various training workshops the question "What makes for a great project manager?" The answers often revolve around management and technical competence. If I have to summarize these competencies into a few requirements in terms of defining the successful project manager, I would list the following:

- Ability to perform beyond the technical parameters of project management
- Ability to see the big picture of the company, not just the details of the project
- Ability to talk the language of the business
- Ability to motivate people in indirect ways to perform a job they may not want to do
- Ability to tie the success of the project to organizational success
- Ability to not get caught up in the doing as opposed to the managing aspects of the job
- Ability to leverage knowledge of past experiences in planning for project risks and avoiding them

The characteristic that distinguishes a great project manager from a good project manager is leadership. The project manager who can elevate his contribution from that of simple management coordination to leadership in the organization is one that provides the ultimate benefit to the organization.

The Project Leadership Model

Leadership is probably one of the most used words in the business language of today. It is also perhaps one of the most misunderstood concepts when it comes to project management.

As I reflect on the various roles that I have held in the profession of project management, I realize that ultimately what leadership means to me is not simply a skill or a piece of information. It is primarily a demonstrable behavior that the individual undertakes in performing a specific job or role in the organization. Leadership is simply action. In fact, without action the word leadership becomes nothing but a cliché within the organization.

In order to attempt to encapsulate the concept of leadership within the action context, there are critical behaviors that distinguish great leaders in project management from the rest of the herd. Each of the project leadership behavior traits has critical inputs that form a link in supporting the individual in attaining this behavior trait. These inputs include:

- **Values:** These are beliefs that the individual leader has which influences the way that this person interacts with the people around them and the environment they live or work in. Beliefs are based on assumptions from the experiences or upbringing that the individual has. Values ultimately tell the story of who we are as humans and what we hold near and dear to our hearts.
- **Know-how:** This is the combination of experience and knowledge that an individual leader possesses. Typically knowledge can either be gained from education or reading that the individual undertakes. Experience comes from both work experience in various roles that individual performs, along with their life experience as far as interacting with family, friends, and colleagues.
- **Skills:** These are capabilities that enable the leader to perform certain tasks or activities. Typically, once an individual develops the knowhow on any given topic or subject, then they can develop the skill or ability to perform an activity. Skills are particularly valuable if they are transferable. In other words, skills that can be applied across industries or jobs.

As I stated, the combination of all of above elements come together to help shape a leader's behavior traits. It is noteworthy here to mention that some inputs (values, know-how, and skills) are applied globally while others may be applied based on the specific situational circumstances. What I mean by globally is not so much in the international arena but rather the idea of holistically. Globally in this sense means that these are traits that are required of a leader regardless of what industry they happen to be in, regardless of the type of project they are managing, and the region of the world they happen to reside or work in. These are traits that are indeed needed no matter what the situation the leader finds themselves in. On the other hand, there are situational traits that are specific to the culture the project is being implemented in or the industry for which the work is being performed. The situational traits are only applicable when certain conditions dictate a necessary skill-set or knowledge area. They may also influence certain values.

One thing to make clear, though, is that this concept is not meant to be a job description for a project manager, nor a formula for identifying the failures of a particular leader. The idea here is to attempt to inform the discussion as to the type of desired characteristics that shape the personality of a leader. Figure 1 is a chart that shows how the model works:

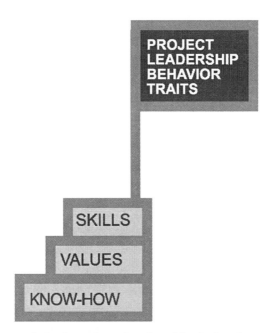

Figure 1. A model of project leadership behavior traits

Within the above mentioned model, there are five project leadership behavior traits that I have identified. They include:

1. Centered on the People
2. Passion for the Mission
3. Obsession with Excellence
4. Imagining and Architecting the Future
5. Focused on Delivery

Each leadership behavior listed above has a set of inputs. These inputs, as I mentioned, can be values, skills, or know-how. There is a strong relationship among the values, skill, and know-how also, which influences how they develop. One value such as acceptance may push an individual to explore developing know-how in the area of building consensus. This, in turn, may lead the person to also acquire listening skills. The way that these values, skill, and knowhow come together also has an impact on the way that the project leadership traits are developed in the person. These behaviors are, after all, a by-product of the convergence of values, skills, and know-how.

In Table 1, I have outlined the details of each of these traits with a specific description of what is meant by the trait, along with the values, skills, and know-how needed as inputs for individual traits.

A true leader in project management is an individual that can demonstrate a strong track record in all of the above behavior traits. Furthermore, these traits have to be tested over time to ensure consistency.

One thing to note, however, is that project leadership must also be based on a mastery of fundamentals. A project manager who is not considered to be a subject matter expert on the topic is not a project manager, which will be the focus on the next chapter.

Within small- and medium-sized organizations, the greatest challenge in dealing with leadership is the ability to foster it

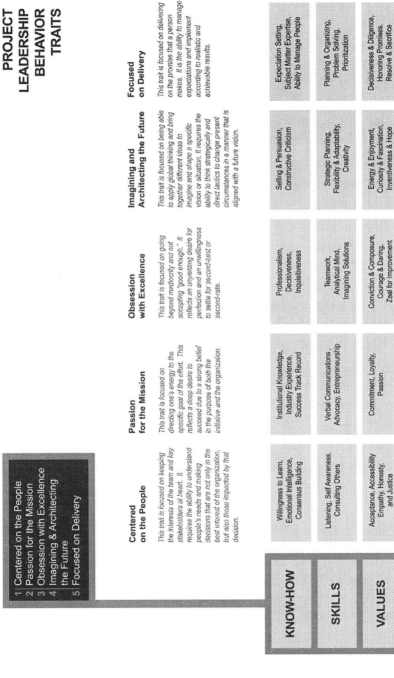

PROJECT LEADERSHIP BEHAVIOR TRAITS

1 Centered on the People
2 Passion for the Mission
3 Obsession with Excellence
4 Imagining & Architecting the Future
5 Focused on Delivery

	Centered on the People	Passion for the Mission	Obsession with Excellence	Imagining and Architecting the Future	Focused on Delivery
	This trait is focused on keeping the interests of the team and key stakeholders at heart. It requires the ability to understand people's needs and making decisions that are not only in the best interest of the organization, but also those impacted by that decision.	*This trait is focused on directing one's energy to the specific goal of the effort. This reflects a deep desire to succeed due to a strong belief in the purpose of both the initiative and the organization.*	*This trait is focused on going beyond mediocrity and not accepting "good enough." It reflects an unyielding desire for perfection and an unwillingness to settle for second-best or second-rate.*	*This trait is focused on being able to apply global thinking and bring together different ideas to imagine and shape a specific vision or situation. It requires the ability to think strategically and direct tactics to change present circumstances in a manner that is aligned with a future vision.*	*This trait is focused on delivering on the promise that a person makes. It is the ability to manage expectations and implement according to realistic and achievable results.*
KNOW-HOW	Willingness to Learn, Emotional Intelligence, Consensus Building	Institutional Knowledge, Industry Experience, Success Track Record	Professionalism, Decisiveness, Inquisitiveness	Selling & Persuasion, Constructive Criticism	Expectation Setting, Subject Matter Expertise, Ability to Manage People
SKILLS	Listening, Self Awareness, Consulting Others	Verbal Communications, Advocacy, Entrepreneurship	Teamwork, Analytical Mind, Imagining Solutions	Strategic Planning, Flexibility & Adaptability, Creativity	Planning & Organizing, Problem Solving, Prioritization
VALUES	Acceptance, Accessibility, Empathy, Honesty, and Justice	Commitment, Loyalty, Passion	Conviction & Composure, Courage & Daring, Zeal for Improvement	Energy & Enjoyment, Curiosity & Fascination, Inventiveness & Hope	Decisiveness & Diligence, Honoring Promises, Resolve & Sacrifice

Table 1. Details of project leadership behavior traits

beyond the most senior management levels in the organization. Typically these organizations lack the financial resources that would enable them to attract the same amount of talent that large organizations do. This is, of course, not to say that small- and medium sized organizations lack talent, but rather their approach to talent management is not nearly as systematic. In family-owned businesses in particular, a glass ceiling often exists for those in the staff ranks who are not related to the owners of the company.

When it comes to the above-outlined project leadership model, the most important element for small- and medium-sized organizations is to understand the interplay between the various inputs that form behavior. Once this is achieved, the leaders of the organization can focus on driving the desired type of behaviors from their employees. Another element that is linked to this is determining whether the organization is required to hire project managers from outside or assign individual performers from within to the role of project manager. While this is certainly related to qualifications in terms of the knowledge of project management and the ability to do the job, another major input to the process should be whether the individual possesses the desired leadership behavior traits or not. If it is determined that the person does not, then it is easy to make a decision on whether it is worth investing the resources to bring them into the organization or provide them the knowledge and/or tools to perform in the job.

6

MASTER THE BASICS

"He who would learn to fly one day must first learn to stand and walk and run and climb and dance; one cannot fly into flying."

Friedrich Nietzsche, German Philosopher

The Fundamentals

In his book *Outliers*, Malcolm Gladwell talks about the 10,000-hour rule. This concept has caught on in business circles. The basic idea is that individuals who have demonstrated excellence in a specific field have done so only after spending at a minimum 10,000 hours practicing and honing their skills. Gladwell uses several examples such as the Beatles, athletes, and other notable personalities to demonstrate and reinforce his point.

As I understand it, the foundational premise of this idea is very simple. If an individual aims to develop strong or advanced skills in a given field, they must put in the time required to help develop this area. The number of hours spent practicing is directly correlated to how good that individual is. While talent certainly plays an important role, however, without practice this person is unlikely to improve and develop.

I believe that there is also another important consideration. This has to do with the way the practice is conducted. If the individual uses proper technique and follows the proper fundamentals of that given field, they are likely to improve; however, if they ignore these fundamentals, they are likely to stagnate. Imagine, for example, children enrolled in a little league sport such as baseball or soccer. If you've ever watched these kids play, you come to a quick realization that much of what is needed at this level is a focus on training the children on the fundamentals of the game. Without developing a basic mastery of these fundamentals, it is unlikely that any of these kids would become good at playing the sport.

In a way, project managers who are in the field are like those kids in little league. A project manager who does not know the basics of the "game" and does not practice them regularly is useless to the team. Also, an organization that does not practice the basics of project management will likely not have a good result when it comes to the projects it undertakes.

This chapter will focus on the basics that must be in place to ensure a greater chance of success on projects and in the adoption of project management practices in small- and medium-sized organizations. I will first look at the basics of project then relate them to programs and portfolios.

The Business Case

Perhaps the most important part of kicking off a project on the right foot is to establish a clear and solid understanding of the business benefits of the initiative and the desired success outcomes in undertaking them.

I have seen several instances where a business case was not developed for a project that ended in failure. Often this happens when an influential executive wants to take on the project, but does not want to spend the time building the business case to justify the expense associated with it.

The business case is a document that highlights the desired outcome and the needed investment for a given project. In my experience, most organizations attempt to include a cost-benefit analysis in the business case.

According to the *PMBOK® Guide,* the business case is usually based on one or more of the following conditions:

- Market demand
- Organizational need
- Customer request
- Technological advance
- Legal requirement
- Ecological impact
- Social need

Building the justification for a project always starts with the articulation of the driving force requiring the project and leads to developing a list of benefits. A good way to look at it is also to ask what will happen if the project is not initiated.

One area for consideration is the role of the cost-benefit analysis in building the business case. Some organizations will insist on the development of a detailed financial model such as a net present value analysis or a calculation like the internal rate of return. The problem that I have encountered in situations where I wanted to develop such models was the fact that in most of the organizations I worked for, very few people understood what I was talking about.

While I had been exposed to these models during my MBA studies, I noticed that even individuals in the finance and accounting departments often lacked the basic understanding to generate this for a project.

In 1998 I was leading a requirements definition process for the implementation of a document management system. The team had a relatively easy time identifying what they liked to see in a system. We were also relatively happy with the cost model that was developed based on market research and vendor input. The challenge for us, however, was a lack of ability to quantify the benefits. We were simply not in a position to turn the benefits into a measurable monetary figure. In the end, we reached an agreement with the project sponsor that the justification would not include a cost-benefit analysis.

In my opinion, most small- and medium-sized organizations are actually not going to be in a position to develop that cost-benefit analysis. The project in the end would be much better served if rigor and focus was given to the qualitative benefits of the project. That's not to say that financial analysis is unimportant, but it may not be realistic for most of these types of organizations.

The Project Charter

A project charter is a document that authorizes the project manager to deploy organizational resources on a given project. It signals the official start of the project and highlights the commitment of the executive sponsor to the parameters of the project.

Developing a project charter for a project of any type and within any sort of organization is a must. Regardless of the size of the company or the type of industry it operates within, the project charter gives legitimacy to the existence of the project.

I like to compare the project charter to a birth certificate. Consider for a moment that a new baby is born and somehow somebody forgot to issue him or her a birth certificate. I suspect that in this situation it is very likely that the baby will not be recognized by the local government, any religious organizations, and in some cases family members.

The key to developing good project charter documents in small- and medium-sized organizations is avoiding complexity and embracing simplicity. Some components that are needed in the project charter include:

- Project goals and objectives (justification)
- Key requirements
- Initial scope definition
- Key deliverables
- Initial staffing and project manager assignment
- Assumptions and constraints

The above items provide for a solid basis or foundation that the project manager can then build upon as they begin the planning cycle with the aid of the team. Furthermore, having this charter ready in time for the team kickoff meeting will help stakeholders to validate their understanding of the project and their expectations of each other and the rest of the organization.

This will be particularly beneficial in trying to establish clarity around the constraints that may be facing the project. By holding discussions with key stakeholders on the charter, the project team will be positioned to flush out any unstated expectations and help the project manager avoid unknown constraints.

The best example that I can think of was related to a customer implementation we were working on while I was with IBM. The client needed us to develop software that would ultimately be used in their manufacturing process. The client, however, did not communicate with us that there was a requirement for having the system operational by a certain date due to legal requirements. Discussions that we had while reviewing the charter helped our implementation team understand that the deadline that the client was imposing on us was not one that came out of thin air but rather a requirement driven by the legal requirements faced by the client.

Scope Definition

One of the most important skills that every project manager must have is the ability to lead his or her team in the development of a work breakdown structure (WBS) for the project. The WBS is a decomposition of the scope of the project divided into work packages based on the deliverables identified by the team.

The WBS allows the project team to apply a systematic approach in identifying all the deliverables of the project and to break them down into the smallest acceptable work packages. The benefit of doing so is that a good WBS can help drive the entire planning process, ranging from effectively setting a baseline to generating a good schedule and budget, as well as identification of barriers and risks.

One thing I want to point out here is that often project management practitioners confuse a work breakdown structure with a schedule. A WBS, is in, fact *not* a schedule as it addresses the "what" of the project and not the "how." The focus in the WBS is primarily to answer the question "What is it that we want to do in this project?" and not "How are we going to accomplish the tasks of the project?"

Another important consideration in developing the WBS is to ensure that any assumptions are clearly documented so as to assist in risk identification and mitigation.

The Project Baseline

One of the first concepts that project management practitioners are introduced to is the triple constraint. Reading through the literature often leads to some confusion as different authors use different "sides" to the triangle.

A triple constraint, simply stated, is a concept that argues that there are three elements to a project that are closely interlinked. I prefer the version of these three items that includes time, cost, and scope, as shown in Figure 2 below.

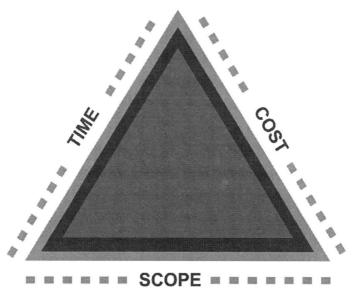

Figure 2. An example of a triple constraint

To better illustrate how the triple constraints interact together, imagine that someone is planning a wedding reception. The parties involved (stakeholders) agreed on the following:

- The wedding reception will be held at a nearby country club
- The groom and the bride will each invite 150 guests
- The wedding will be held in six months

Each of the above statements, in itself, defines one side of the triangle but also greatly influences at least one more side of the triangle. As stated, the fact that there will be 300 invited guests means that there is a defined cost associated with them. It also has influence on the venue as the venue must hold that number of guests. Similarly, the choice of the country club requires that it can accommodate 300 guests but also has influence on the cost associated with the reception. The fact that the wedding needs to be held in six months adds that third constraint, dictating the timeline and requiring a specific expectation.

As you can imagine, if one element of the above changes, it is very likely that this change will influence another side of that triangle to change.

Using the above example may seem a bit basic but would likely make understanding the triple constraint concept fairly straightforward. Yet in so many organizations, of all sizes and types, I have seen management often dictate every single aspect of this triangle. I remember in one project the sponsor told us that we had to add three more deliverables to the project (increasing the scope side) and we had to finish two months ahead of schedule (reducing the time side). He then stated that we had to do it with the same exact budget. Now imagine if you were attempting to change the size of two of the sides without changing the third. It is physically impossible.

Organizations should always strive to allow the project manager to manage and control the project within the triple constraints

If, in fact, there are driving forces that require fixing one or two of the sides, the organization needs to develop enough maturity to allow the project manager authority and control over the third. Otherwise, the project is set up for failure.

The benefit of understanding the triple constraint within the context of the project allows the project manager to establish the baseline for the project when it comes to scope, time, and cost. This will be the initial marker in judging the success of the project.

The Project Management Plan

If a project charter is like a birth certificate for a project, then the project plan is like the college savings plan the parents might buy for their baby to enhance their ability to send him or her to college.

The project management plan is a document developed by the project manager in coordination with the team and by the approval of the executive sponsor. The plan lays out a framework for managing, controlling, and implementing the project.

Having traveled the world advocating on behalf of PMI and project management, I have observed that whenever our ideas and standards encountered resistance, it would often start with a misconception around planning. I remember a keynote speech in Warsaw at the PMI Research Conference in 2008 while I was Chairman of the Institute. My speech was focused on how project management as a profession and our standards in general can serve as a common language for bringing people together and helping professionals and organizations prosper. At the conclusion of the speech, there was a break and as I was walking toward the door to go to the next activity an attendee caught me to chat and get introduced. The first thing that he said was that he worked in an organization that was new to project management and his senior leadership team were not supportive of adopting our standards because "our methodology" was too rigid.

That statement caught my attention and I wanted to immediately respond with a comment about how the *PMBOK®
Guide* and the framework it contains is a standard and not a
methodology. However, I stopped myself for a change and allowed him the opportunity to talk. I started to understand where
his confusion was coming from. So many new project managers,
in their zeal to be *"PMBOK® Guide* compliant" end up overdoing the planning process. It is almost as though they think that
their performance is being graded by the weight and length of
the project plan. Indeed there is not an understanding that the
standard provides a guideline on how a project management
plan can be developed, but it is not prescriptive in the sense of
providing a template with required fields.

A good project management plan is one that first captures
the scope, cost, and time baseline of the project. These elements are a must to help define the major parameters of the
project. However, the way the timeline is portrayed has to
reflect the requirements of the organization and the project. In
some small companies, it may be that the project schedule is
nothing but a high-level list of deliverables and expected dates
for completion.

In addition to articulating the triple constraint elements, it
is a wise idea for the plan to address how the project management team will administer activities such as communications,
procurement, human resources, quality, and risk. However,
these sections don't necessarily have to be complex in structure and long in detail. The important thing in this process is to
allow for relevant detail to be documented and communicated
with project stakeholders.

The Executive Sponsor and Steering Committees

One mistake I made early in my career was to focus too much
on cost, time, and scope, at the expense of focusing on key

stakeholder interactions. The project management plan must highlight how the project manager will interact with key stakeholders such as the project sponsor and a steering/approval committee.

During the life cycle of a given project, there will be points where the project manager will find themselves having to communicate progress, explain issues, or secure approval for changes or deliverables. It is important from the beginning that the project manager takes into consideration how these interactions are defined.

Even later in my career, I struggled to give this enough focus. I recall on a project I was managing while I was at IBM we had a client who was anxious to get started on the project. As a result, we did what we normally do, which was insert language in the statement of work related to how deliverables were to be approved. This is standard language that most IBM client projects will have.

The language effectively says something like "Once a deliverable is completed, it is submitted to the client for review and feedback. . . . If the client does not provide feedback within five days, the deliverable is considered approved."

Unfortunately, we did not spend enough time with the client on the front end going over this language and establishing clearer criteria for approving deliverables. Once the project manager from the client side had a chance to read through the SOW, he freaked out. He sent me an e-mail saying that if we insisted on this and did not give the client organization more time in reviewing the deliverable, then he would be forced to reject every single deliverable out of hand.

As you can see, this behavior and interaction could put the entire project at risk. Had we discussed this issue with the client prior to the start of the project, we might have reached a better compromise.

Processes that need definition as part of the project management plan may include:

- Deliverable review and approval
- Test exit criteria
- Change request submittal, review, and approval
- Issue resolution and negotiations
- Phase gate reviews
- Requirements review and approval

Each of the above-mentioned items, along with others, may have a different process with different stakeholders requiring participation. This is often driven by the organization, as far as who is involved in which activity. In some small organizations, it may be that there is no need for a steering committee and an expectation that the sponsor will approve or deliberate on some of these items.

I have found a simple tool such as a RACI chart with a line for each stakeholder offers significant value to the process.

- **R**esponsible
- **A**ccountable
- **C**onsulted
- **I**nformed

Other organizations may even want to include groups that are not directly involved in the project but are greatly impacted by the product of the project. An example of this is the end users of a software development project or the tenants of a building that just finished its construction phase.

Closeout

Yet another important consideration is the need to properly close out projects. I often ask my workshop participants the question

"How many of you participated in projects, within your organization, that were not closed out." I remember one participant saying that "projects in our company don't end. They die a miserable, slow death, and on the way everyone in the company stops paying any attention to them."

Unfortunately, small- and medium-sized organizations that do not have a formal approach to approving the funding of projects often fall prey to this issue. Establishing the needed discipline to bring the project to closure allows the team to capture important lessons learned and best practices as a result of their experiences on the project. It also allows the project manager to bring to a finality all open issues and items. Finally, closeout allows the organization the ability to celebrate success and thank the team for their hard work and effort.

Beyond Projects and into Portfolios

The entire focus of the previous sections within this chapter has been on effective "project" management. However, an important consideration is that projects in organizations often are not stand-alone animals. They exist within the context of many projects that sometimes form programs or an entire portfolio of projects.

Small- and mid-sized organizations must not only develop the discipline for managing projects one at a time, but also must develop a system for managing the portfolio of projects, and in some instances programs.

A portfolio is multiple projects and/or programs that are managed collectively and in a way that helps enhance the organization's ability to align them to organizational objectives. It is also important to note that these projects and programs may or may not be interdependent or directly related.

Some of the important lessons learned that I have captured over the years in terms of positioning the organization for success in this area include the following:

- **Focus on the professionals and not the process.** In other words, sometimes the size of the organization or its culture do not allow for a very rigorous process to be implemented in managing portfolios. This can be especially true as management attempts to evaluate competing projects and allocate funding. In this case, it is important for the organization to seek solid professionals and position them in the role of project management practitioners. These people need to be veterans who are capable of working independently as opposed to being totally dependent on following someone else's process.

- **Focus on principles, not on methodology.** Many small- and medium-sized organizations do not have the wherewithal to develop detailed methodology or even simply adopt them. Project managers in such organizations find themselves either stuck with implementing another company's methodology that is not suited to their organization, or they become frustrated that no standard can ever be followed. It is important for the leaders responsible for the practice of project management in the organization sit down with key executives and develop a list of "strategic principles" that the organization can agree on for its portfolio. These principles can either be worded as constraints or opportunities. An example could be something like "any project with an anticipated budget of less than $50,000 does not require a project plan."

- **Focus on the strategic priorities.** The process for managing projects, programs, and portfolios within the organization should also take into account strategic priorities as defined in the organization's vision and strategy.

If, for example, the organization prides itself on being flexible and dynamic, that will have a huge impact on how various project management processes are designed and managed.

- **The need for standardization.** Another element that is critical in standardization is to ensure consistency in measuring progress on initiatives. Standardizing monitoring reports is a step in the right direction. Executives must be able to compare "apples to apples." If there are multiple project managers, each with their own process and template, this only creates confusion in the organization.

- **Approval cycles.** Executive teams in small- and medium-sized organizations must also be trained on how to manage the review and approval cycle related to portfolios, especially when it comes to phase gates. There is nothing worse than having a project team wait for weeks on end to receive approval to move on to the next phase of a program.

Mastering the basics of project management, whether on a single project, a program, or a portfolio of projects, is easy in theory. However, one must take into account other elements such as culture, people, and buy-in.

One must not forget that the organization must have in place the necessary support elements to enable project management practitioners the maximum chance for success. Having necessary tools in place will enhance a greater understanding of the work that project practitioners perform. This will be the focus of the next chapter.

7

TOOL TIME

"Things should be as simple as possible,
but not simpler."

Albert Einstein, Theoretical Physicist, Philosopher and Author

One of the very first expressions that I heard from a veteran project manager was "a fool with a tool is just a fool." Unfortunately I have seen several examples during my career where this expression was not disproved but rather embraced.

Many new entrants into the world of project management assume that the moment they begin to use a tool like Microsoft Project, they will become masterful project managers. Sadly, nothing could be further from the truth.

Consider a person who is interested in becoming a novelist. This person perhaps has always been intrigued by writing and wants a career in this field. To support this interest, this person goes out, buys a new laptop along with a copy of a word processing software.

After installing the word processing software and spending weeks learning how to use it, this individual comes to a very harsh realization. This realization is that the laptop and word processing application have taught him nothing about writing. In fact he is no better a writer than when he started the process. After all, purchasing Microsoft Word does not make a person a writer; it simply makes them the proud owner of a product license.

Similarly, a person who either buys a project management tool such as software or is exposed to some sort of training on a scheduling program should not expect that they will become a good project manager. In fact, they are likely to get lost on the good practice of project management.

Having said all this, however, there are some tools that can simplify the process once the person develops a solid foundation in knowledge of project management. These instruments become part of the project management practitioner's tool box to better enable them to perform their duties.

For illustration purposes, I will use a simple case study of a company that has experienced a certain amount of growth in the market. The accounting manager has highlighted the potential need for the company to upgrade its financial systems from an off-the-shelf product into a more configurable financial package. Furthermore, I will divide these tools into categories that fit within the five process groups of project management: Initiating, Planning, Executing, Monitoring and Controlling, and Closing.

Prior to looking at some of these tools in depth, I want to also mention that the organization has to consider a few things when it comes to tools.

- **Complexity:** Does the organization has processes already in place that are fairly complex when it comes to managing functions such as finance and human resources. Will the introduction of project management practices interface with the other processes in the organization?
- **Scalability:** Where will all the project, program, and portfolio documentation be housed and shared with key organizational stakeholders? Will there be a need to share information quickly and with large groups? Will the organization use the information for future planning purposes?
- **Maturity:** How mature is the practice of project management in the organization? Are there veteran project managers who have been working in the organization for a while?

The answers to these questions will have a dramatic impact on how tools are rolled out in the organization. They also will lead to decisions like whether to build tools internally or go out and buy them from vendors in the field.

Let me start, though, with some basic definitions to help inform the discussion. A tool is a tangible instrument that is used in building or assisting in the creation of the deliverables of the project. This could be a template, software program, or working method. Templates, in this case, are particularly helpful as they are usually a standardized form that is partially filled out with a specific format and structure.

For the purposes of this book, I will make the assumption that most small- and medium-sized organizations are at the beginning of the road in their maturity of implementing the practice of project management. As such, they will likely not be ready for the implementation of project management software at the enterprise level such as Primavera or MS Project Enterprise tools.

It may become obvious after the organization begins practicing project management that such tools are needed to achieve a level of effectiveness that may not be achievable with simple tools and templates. However, I will not spend time discussing these tools, as there are powerful tools that can easily be manually implemented and managed in a simple folder structure that can be just as helpful to the small- and medium-sized organization. These tools are templates that project management practitioners can use in delivering value to the organization.

Pre-Initiation Tools

Project Selection Template: I have observed many small- and medium-sized organizations struggle with the concept of project selection. There are many challenges that they face that make this process even more difficult, including:

- Limited resources and budget that can be assigned to multiple projects.
- Too many projects get commissioned at the same time.
- Lack of a centralized process for evaluating projects across the entire business before approving their budget.

An initiative evaluation form assists the organization in standardizing the process for evaluating projects. It can be applied to projects that come before an evaluation committee to guide their decisions on granting funding.

The committee typically would apply criteria for evaluating proposed initiatives ranging from strategic alignment to legal requirements. Table 2 is a sample that highlights potential criteria as well as a suggested simple framework for rating.

Project Name	Accounting System Implementation		
Project Description	The existing finance and accounting package no longer meets the organization's needs. A new system must be identified and implemented		
Champion	The accounting manager		
Criteria	Weight	Rating	Score
Provides Good Return on Investment	0.3	5	1.5
Supports Organizational Strategy	0.3	10	3
Advances Customer Relationships	0.2	5	1
Improves Internal Processes	0.1	5	0.5
Enhances Employee Performance	0.1	0	0
Total			6

Table 2. Sample initiative evaluation form

The criteria may be defined based on organizational needs and often differ from one year to the next, depending on annual organizational priorities. For organizations that are looking to implement a planning process, this table is ideal, as it rates the project against criteria, taking into account the level of importance of each criteria. The rating is multiplied by the weight and the score is added up for a final total.

The organization may decide, for instance, that any potential project that scores 5 or below would automatically be disqualified from proceeding further. Another important consideration is to provide guidance on how the rating should take place. For example, on the criteria related to return on investment, the organization may decide the use a systematic approach with a calculation such as internal rate of return (IRR). In this instance, the raters may be given direction to the effect that if the IRR is less than 8%, the rating should be 0; if it is between 8% and 10%, it should be 5; and if it is above 10%, it should be 10. The key is to establish some consistency in terms of evaluating potential projects to ensure that the organization is comparing apples to apples rather than apples to oranges.

Project Prioritization Template: Once the proposed project passes the selection process, that does not necessarily mean that the organization will initiate work on it. Typically, the selection template tells the organization whether a project is worthwhile or not. The prioritization template is beneficial because it assists the organization in identifying which of the selected projects are more important than others. The intent of this template is to evaluate projects against each other to determine which ones have a higher degree of importance to the organization. Experience has taught me that organizations find it almost impossible to eliminate subjectivity as part of the process. So rather than fight it, another approach, as illustrated by the example shown in Table 3, would be to embrace it.

	Impact on Company	Chances of Success	Total (Multiplied)	Executive Committee Ranking
Accounting System Implementation	2	3	6	1
Company Expansion to New City	3	1	3	3
New Product Launch	3	2	6	2
Office Parking Lot Improvement	1	2	2	5
Creating a new Department	2	1	2	4

Table 3. A matrix for prioritizing approved projects

Once the prioritization is performed, the organization is then in the position to identify which projects should be initiated immediately and which ones must be delayed or put on hold.

It is, however, important to mention that the above tool does not take into consideration complexity stemming from project cash flow, scope, time, and budget. It may be that the first priority that was identified above is a project that cannot start until a time that is later than a second priority. Another issue that the tool does not address is project dependencies. It may be the case that Project B has to be completed in order to begin Project A. These details have to be taken into account as part of the process.

Initiation Tool

In the previous chapter, I described the importance of the project charter document in laying out the scope of the project and the authority of the project manager. The project charter as a document is usually produced by the sponsor of the project.

Another very effective tool that can be used by project teams and organizations is a statement of work template (SOW). An SOW is a document that provides a detailed narrative of the products and services to be delivered by the performing organization. It also highlights the nature of the relationship between the customer and the performing organization.

Often an SOW is developed as a subsidiary agreement under a master agreement such as a contract between the client and service provider.

Consider based on our example that the given company has selected a software solution for their accounting system. Table 4 shows an illustration of the key sections that could be included in the statement of work template between the vendor and the company.

Statement of Work		
Scope of Work	*This section describes the work to be performed under this agreement. The scope of this project includes the implementation of the selected accounting system, including documenting specifications, deploying the new system, and migrating historical data to the system.*	
Agreement Parameters	*Defines the parties entering the agreement, staffing requirements for the project, and requirements associated with delivering the project.*	
	The following staff will be needed for the project:	
	Vendor - Project Manager - IT Architect - 2 Developers - 1 Tester - 1 Business Analyst	Customer - Project Manager - Business Subject Matter Expert - 2 Users
Deliverables	*Description of the products and services delivered on the project.*	
	- The system must be implemented prior to the end of the year. - Management has allocated $100k for the project - The chart of accounts will remain the same - The team will use system functionality that exists in the solution and will not customize the product - Additional hardware will be needed to house the system	
Key Assumptions	*This describes the agreed upon assumptions. If these items change, then the parameters of the agreement could be changed.*	
	- Project Plan, including schedule and budget - System Requirements - Implementation Specifications - Deployment - Data Migration - Training - Documentation	
Roles and Responsibilities	*This describes the agreed upon assumptions. If these items change, then the parameters of the agreement could be changed.*	
	Vendor will be responsible for: - Requirements validation - Detailed system design and implementation guide - System configuration - System deployment - Training and documentation - Data migration	Customer will be responsible for: - Providing business subject matter expertise - Meeting participation - Hardware procurement and initial setup - Knowledge transfer - Providing resources for training

Table 4. Sample of a statement of work

Statement of Work *(continued)*

Financial Arrangement	*This section describes the charges, fees, and expenses to be charged to the client. It may also include a payment schedule.*
	The agreed-upon fees as define in the contract include $50,000 for software and $50,000 for consulting and implementation services. The payment schedule will be as follows: - 20% upon SOW signing - 30% upon plan approval - 30% upon system deployment - 20% upon data migration completion
Change Control	*This section provides for an outline of how changes are to be handled on the project.*
	Change will be managed in accordance with the approved procedure as defined in the change request template.
Duration of Agreement	*Outlines the details of the timeline along with a high-level milestone chart.*
	- Week 0 - Initiation - Week 2 - System Requirements - Week 5 - Implementation Specifications - Week 10 - Deployment - Week 14 - Data Migration - Week 16 - Training - Week 18 – Documentation - Week 20 - Closeout This agreement is good for 1 year.
Confidentiality and IP	*Defines the confidentially parameters along with the intellectual property rights of the deliverables completed in the agreement.*
	Source code is owned by the vendor and accounting data is owned by the customer.
Signatures	*Signatures of parties entering the agreement.*

Table 4. (*Continued*)

Planning Tools

When it comes to planning, the work breakdown structure (WBS) must always be the beginning point. In the last chapter, I explained how the WBS could be used in the small- and medium-sized organization. This is one of the basics of project management, as is the importance of managing the triple constraint of time, cost, and scope. Having proper documentation of the scope, along with a detailed schedule and budget is critical in terms of planning. Scheduling software offers more than adequate help in building the necessary plans for the timeline and budget.

The tools that I would like to highlight here, however, are templates that are not usually addressed in software like scheduling tools.

Human Resources: project staffing is an important element in planning. Table 5 outlines a simple way of capturing staffing requirements for the project example that is being used in this chapter:

Resource Information	Resource 1	Resource 2	Resource 3
Role *This describes the role that the individual will pay on the project*	Project Manager	IT Architect	Software Developer
Authority and Accountability *This identifies the level of authority and accountability provided to this individual*	This person is the project team leader and is authorized with managing team activities and approving deliverables	This person is responsible for leading the technical resources	This person is responsible for system development

Table 5. Staffing requirements chart

Resource Information	Resource 1	Resource 2	Resource 3
Responsibilities *This defines the duties assigned to this person in performing the work on the project*	- Facilitates team to create plan - Manages change control - Manages deliverable approval	- Approves technical design - Signs off on technical deployment - Is responsible for quality assurance	- Is responsible for application development - Is responsible for documentation - Participates in user training
Level of Commitment *This specifies the amount of time that this resource will dedicate to the project*	100% for the duration of the project	75% for the duration of the project	100% for the duration of the project

Table 5. (*Continued*)

Completing Table 5 accurately will enable the project manager to understand each person's role so that the team can work effectively together. Having clarity around each person's responsibilities will also help in building a good schedule and timeline and will ensure that the team members are holding each other accountable, as they will be dependent on each other in the delivery of the project.

As part of this table, it is also beneficial to clarify the level of authority that each team member has when it comes to processes such as approving deliverables and project plans.

Risk: Risk planning starts with an identification of the risk events followed by quantification and response planning. The template shown in Table 6 offers a simple way for addressing these processes:

Risk Event	Probability	Impact	Score	Risk Response	Action Plan
Description					
This is a description of the potential risk condition and the timing associated of when it might occur	*An assigned number that identifies if the likelihood of the risk event occurring is a low, medium, or high*	*This is attempting to capture if the result of the risk occurring will have a low, medium, or high impact on the project*	*This is a multiplication of the probability and impact*	*A decision reflecting the organizational criteria to either accept, mitigate, or transfer the risk event*	*These are steps that should be taken to address the risk based on the response strategy*
Sample Risk Event associated with implementing the accounting system					
Trainer not being available during implementation	Low = 1	High = 10	Score = 10	Mitigate	Identify potential backup in case of emergency

Table 6. Risk planning template

As part of the risk planning process, the project team has to determine what the organizational risk tolerance is so that an agreement can be reached on which risks the team will ultimately accept.

Risks always take place within the context of a time and it is important as part of the planning process that the team identify the "risk event," which includes the potential risk along with when this risk might take place. Establishing an understanding of this is important in drafting risk response strategies and action plans.

Action plans should include the steps necessary to overcome the risk along with identifying the specific triggers that will help the team identify if and when this risk has taken place. The risk may be assigned to a team member to observe with the responsibility to alert the organization if they see certain triggers taking place.

Communications: interacting with stakeholders effectively forms a solid foundation for project success. The template in Table 7 highlights a simple tactical plan for addressing communications with project stakeholders:

STAKEHOLDER COMMUNICATIONS

WHAT	WHEN	WHO	WHOM	HOW
Information outlining the specific message to be communicated.	The person responsible for initiating the communication.	The frequency of the communication and the timeline for its delivery.	The receivers of the communication.	The medium for communicating the message.
Sample: Project status report	*Sample:* The project manager	*Sample:* Every Friday throughout the project lifecycle	*Sample:* Executive sponsor, steering committee, project team	*Sample:* E-mail, team intranet

Table 7. Sample template for stakeholder communications

The tool shown in Table 7 helps the team identify key messages that needs to be communicated throughout the project life cycle, along with the key stakeholder involved in the communication process. It would include as many communication vehicles as appropriate for the project in its organization.

Execution Tools

Logs: Upon approval of the project plan and authorization of the charter elements of scope, time, and cost, the project manager is responsible for overseeing delivery activities. A very valuable element in this process is maintaining a handle on project activities. This is often best performed with a log. Table 8 is a sample log table that identifies the major elements for tracking purposes:

#	Description	Category	Owner	Approver	Open On	Due	Status
1	Charter Submitted	Decision Point	Executive Sponsor	Steering Committee	Feb 3	Mar 15	Closed
2	Update the Project Schedule	Action Item	Project Manager	Executive Sponsor	Mar 17	Mar 31	Com-pleted
3	A problem with the version of software used in development	Issue	Software Developer	IT Architect	Apr 15	TBD	Open

Table 8. Sample project activity log

It is also noteworthy to mention that there might be a need to maintain multiple logs for the project. The project manager may have a separate log for the following:

- Issues log
- Risk log
- Decision log
- Change log

Often the complexity of the project along with parameters such as time and scope will dictate how these will be formatted.

Status Reporting: One of the most important functions that the project manager takes care of during the execution of the project is communicating status to stakeholders. It is important that this process take place in a manner that meets the needs of the organization. I have often seen status reports that are too complex or long for any executive sponsor to understand. The template in Table 9 is intended as a sample that offers basic, simple information. The top right corner gives the project manager an opportunity to check a status of "red," "yellow," or "green" for the project. The key to remember is that the status report is an invitation to engage stakeholders in dialogue on the project.

PROJECT NAME: Customer Relationship Management Deployment					
Project Summary Scope: Customer Relationship Management Deployment			**Targeted Start**	**Targeted Finish**	
Deliverables:			**Major Milestones**		
1. System			**Milestone**	**Date**	
2. Training			Customization	Mar 1	
3. Documentation			Installation	Mar 30	
Project Value:			Training	Apr 30	CONFIDENTIAL
$100K			Cutover	May 15	
			Closeout	May 30	
Resource Allocation					
Name	**Roles**	**Date Needed**	**Date Released**	**% Commitment**	
R1	Project Manager	Feb 1	May 30	100%	
R2	IT Developer	Mar 1	May 30	100%	
R3	Business Analyst	Feb 1	May 30	50%	
Major Issues/ Risks					
• Business analyst required to transition out of project earlier than expected • No documentation specialist has been assigned					

Table 9. Status report template

Another set of tools that may be applied in addition to templates are process descriptions that highlight the procedure for a given activity within the project. An example of this could be the deliverable approval processes as shown in Figure 3:

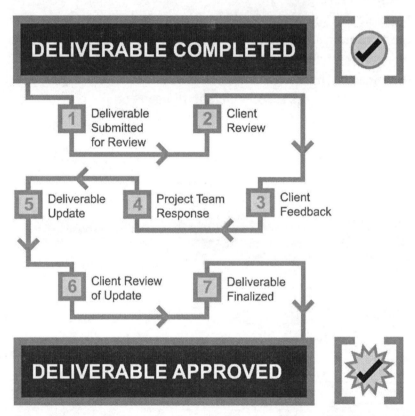

Figure 3. Sample process description for deliverable approval

Controlling Tools

Change control is focused on identifying potentially necessary deviations from the scope, cost, and time of the project baseline, determining if they should be approved or rejected, and

Number	Serial Number	Sample Change
Description	*Define the required change that is needed on the project*	The team identified that the number of user licenses is not enough as they discovered a need in the HR department to have access to certain functionality
Justification	*Identify the reasons that prompted the submission of this request*	This change is important to ensure meeting departmental requirements
Initiator	*Identify the person or organization requesting the change*	IT Architect
Impact	*What is the exact impact of the change in terms of scope, time, cost?*	The cost of user licenses and training 2 additional users
Analysis	*Has qualitative or quantitative analysis been performed in support of this request?*	An additional $5000 is needed
Input	*Has input from the various stakeholders been solicited and if so, what was the feedback?*	Project team reviewed and project manager recommends change
Decision	*Approve/Reject*	APPROVED

Table 10. Change-control template

managing them in a proactive manner. A change control request template is one that can help stakeholders understand the driving forces behind the change and the needed analysis prior to making a decision. The template should include the information as shown in Table 10.

Closeout Tools

I mentioned in the previous chapter that one of the most important activities for the project manager is the process of closing out the project. There are several tools that can be used at this stage. One template that can prove beneficial is a project evaluation form. This document can take the shape of a log that captures lessons learned and best practices. Table 11 shows a sample list of the data elements that could be captured in this document.

#	Project Accomplishment	Lessons Learned	Intellectual Property Created
	Describe the milestones achieve, deliverables created, and the skills acquired	*Identify the issues encountered and how they were resolved, the risks that were mitigated, and the actions taken*	*Define the best practices that were captured and identify the assets that were harvested on the project*
1	Deployment completed on time	Not all users were identified but this only resulted in additional cost	Process captured and communicated with departmental stakeholders
2	Training completed	A dry run for the training should have been held	Documentation transitioned to customer
3	Data Migrated	Initial inconsistencies were discovered and backup was used to restore	System configuration transitioned

Table 11. Sample lessons-learned log

Tools Conclusion

In addition to the above-mentioned templates, there are other templates that may be useful to small- and medium-sized organizations. They could include those for:

- Business case development
- Requirements definition
- Timesheet reporting
- Project auditing
- Meeting minutes and notes creation

The most important nugget of wisdom that I learned is that the most valuable tool is the brain of the project management practitioner, which is needed in leveraging this tool box. As long as there is consistency in the process, stakeholders will know what to expect.

8

DEFINE SUCCESS

"Would you like me to give you a formula for success? It's quite simple, really. Double your rate of failure. You are thinking of failure as the enemy of success. But it isn't at all. You can be discouraged by failure or you can learn from it, So go ahead and make mistakes. Make all you can. Because remember that's where you will find success."

Thomas J. Watson, IBM Founder

The above quote rings so true because most small- and medium-sized organizations find themselves in one of two positions. The first is one where managers and leaders throw caution to the wind and ignore risks and fears. The second is that they develop an unhealthy fear of everything, especially failure, and in the process set the stage to avoid success all together.

During my first few months with Blue Cross and Blue Shield of Louisiana, the company was attempting to make a turnaround after it had been put under government supervision. As it turns out, there were a few executives in the organization who were abusing power and the state came in and enforced a change in the board of directors and management of the organization. Perhaps in today's economic climate with the government's significant investment in the private sector this may not be a huge issue, but in the mid 1990s this was major news in the state of Louisiana.

I joined the company shortly after the new state-appointed CEO took over. The CEO had made changes to the executive team that included the appointment of a vice president in charge of compliance. This vice president was responsible effectively to clean house, which she did. The beauty of the job that she was given was the sheer amount of power and influence she had in the company.

It was made clear that those who did not cooperate 100 percent were to be removed immediately. There was no choice and as a result, people feared for their job and did as they were asked.

The new CEO and the executive team worked hard to pull the company out of state supervision and quickly demonstrated their strength to the market. The success exhibited in this story would perhaps lead the reader to the wrong assumption. Those wrong assumptions are that fear tactics work, and that success comes from avoiding failure.

Nothing could be further from the truth, in fact, than those two statements. Those who witnessed this period in the company's history know that any success was due to the teamwork and dedication of the employees who genuinely cared about the company. Yes, it is true that some were motivated out of fear of losing their job, but the market as a whole was booming and for anyone who felt that fear, they could have easily gotten a job elsewhere

In reflecting on some of the discussions that I had with our management team at the time, I cannot help but admire the vision that the vice president of compliance brought to the organization. In a manner of months, she transformed her job from control to facilitation. She capitalized on the creation of her new department, built up several functions in the organization such as strategic planning and project management, and reached out to the entire executive team requesting participation and input.

During a conversation with her, she had joked about the fact that fear of failure at one point in the organization was silly. She told me that she was happy to challenge anybody in the organization to name a single person who was fired because of failure. The fear of failing leads to only one thing—lack of trying. When the individual is afraid, they are less likely to take a chance on success.

Defining Success

It may be relatively easy for some organizations to define success in terms of financial measures. Public companies, in particular, are not only under the spotlight when it comes to measuring things like earnings per share, but they also find it critical to keep score of how they're doing as compared to others.

Financial success, however, has often been confused with real success. Over the past decade, several models have emerges to help blend the concept of financial success with other measures. Most notable, of course, is the Balanced Scorecard Model by Robert Kaplan and David Norton.

In this model, Kaplan and Norton demonstrate that there are other objectives for an organization besides the purely financial ones. These include objectives related to customers, internal processes, and learning and growth.

The Balanced Scorecard recognizes that success is multi-dimensional, and, as such, has to be looked at from different angles. Similarly, organizations that might be in the not-for-profit or government sector, or those who have a different ownership structure, may seek to customize the definition of success to take into consideration things like impact on society or the environment.

Project Success

While much has been written about success, the thing that is clear to me is that success means different things to different people. This is especially true when one is attempting to measure performance and success in the area of project management. Consider, for a moment, the potential criteria that have to be taken into account when trying to build a success measurement model:

- Achieving goals of the strategic plan
- Delivering projects on time
- Executing initiatives under budget
- Meeting the scope of a project
- Satisfying both stated and unstated needs of the customer

The above items are enough to send the sane person into the depths of confusion, now imagine adding yet another layer of complexity to include not only projects but also programs and portfolios.

A few years ago, studies showed that the rate of project failure was staggeringly high. One study I saw indicated that 80% of IT projects fail. However, what does that exactly mean? How did they fail and according to what definition?

Perhaps the issue is that project management practitioners are a bit on the pessimistic side. Maybe they see the glass half empty instead of half full. So rather than saying "Sorry, we delivered your project six months late," it might behoove them to say "Congratulations, you just saved six months of maintenance costs from your project budget."

Unlimited Resources

In 1997, I was attending the PMI global conference in Chicago. One presentation that caught my attention was a case study of the great pyramids at Giza. The presenter, who has since became a close friend, was highlighting how the builders of these pyramids were applying the principles of project management thousands of years prior to the existence of the *PMBOK® Guide.* In essence, he was saying that the builders understood triple constraints long before project management became a profession.

Interestingly enough during the question and answer session, one of the participants challenged his view by saying that the builders did not use project management principles for one simple reason—the Pharaoh had unlimited resources at his disposal. Indeed, what use would the ancient Egyptians have for the triple constraint theory when they did not have to worry about money?

My friend's response was both humorous and wise. He said that while there were clear indications that money was, in fact, limited, he will not argue the point. He pointed to another side of the triangle and that's time. He asked the commenter, what would happen if Pharaoh died prior to the completion of the pyramid? Wouldn't you have considered that project a failure? Obviously, time was of critical importance.

This story again highlights the different paradigms that people have regarding success. Most project managers are trained to think of success in terms of on time and under budget. However, life is a bit more complicated.

Success or Failure?

When it comes to defining success, I have often heard the story of the Sydney Opera House. When the Sydney Opera house was commissioned, there appeared to be a difference in expectations between what was initially promised and the final result.

The project was delivered grossly over budget and significantly behind schedule. In some respects, the magnitude of deviation could easily point out that this perhaps is one of the most poorly management projects in history.

Ironically, the Sydney Opera House as a landmark is one of the most recognizable icons in the world. It is a point of national pride for Australians and a true marvel to look at. The enduring nature of the structure itself ultimately overshadowed the performance of the project during construction.

The truth of the matter is in some cases being under budget and within schedule is not relevant to the overall objective of the project. Success, like beauty, is often in the eyes of the beholder.

View of Success

Defining success on projects is not a simple process, since time and money (both of which are important) are not the only parameters that should be considered. The project management practitioner ultimately has to lead the team in painting a picture of success. Oftentimes, what helps is to start asking the team questions. These questions can include:

- What does success on this project/program/portfolio look like?
- How do we know that we have achieved success?
- Are there multiple measures of success, and if so, what are they?
- What happens when the project fails in some respects but succeeds in others?
- Do different stakeholders have a different view of success?

It will become evident once the team begins to answer these questions that the most important element in achieving success is to rally the team to one definition of success as opposed to two or five or 10 different perspectives or versions of success.

From Complexity to Success

In a speech addressing a joint session of the U.S. Congress in 1961, President Kennedy announced a dramatic and ambitious goal of sending an American safely to the moon before the end of that decade.

While this goal established an amazing vision that most Americans immediately identified with, it presented a challenge since the United States did not possess the technology and skillset to make it happen in 1961.

Often we find ourselves in this exact situation. Projects grow out of someone's vision with little thought as to whether it is realistic. The job of the project management practitioner is to lead the team in defining the success measures to ensure that the vision is realized.

Building the Success Narrative

The best way to illustrate how the project manager can facilitate the team in achieving success for the project is to rely on a scenario that one company I worked with encountered a few years ago. A client of our organization who owned an automobile dealership hired our consulting team to assist him in his expansion efforts.

The CEO of this organization had signed an agreement with an automobile manufacturer to import their cars into his country. As part of that deal, he had committed to creating a healthy brand representation with 10 dealership locations around the country. Our team's scope was to manage the project on behalf of the client and interface with third-party contractors to ensure that these 10 locations were built according to specification.

As the project unfolded and the team began work on the activities, the project manager started to run into major issues with the client. During one session, the client CEO articulated a lack of satisfaction with the leadership skills of the project manager. He provided the example that the project manager did not do a good job in selecting a certain location for one of the dealership sites. When I later spoke with the project manager, he informed me that this was not his job but rather the marketing manager's job.

Right off the bat it was clear that we had a mismatch of expectations, and I believe that the primary cause of this was a lack of definition around project success. Following the incident with the project manager and CEO, the team struggled for a few additional months until the project came to a conclusion.

Having had the benefit of a few years' reflection, I have thought about how I would have approached this project had I been involved from the beginning. Below are the steps that I would have taken to help facilitate a joint definition of success:

- **Business objectives.** This first step in the process is to try and understand what the project goals are and what business objectives need to be achieved. This is much like trying to establish clarity regarding an organizational vision. In this example, the business objective was fairly straightforward. It was to build out 10 dealership locations according to pre-defined specifications.
- **Project stakeholders.** Once the business objectives are understood, it is important to identify who the project stakeholders are. The best way of doing this is to conduct interviews with the various executives and team members. I have found that the initial set of stakeholders identified

by clients is never a complete list. You might find that one group will lead to identification of another group. Talking with stakeholders will help clarify their interest. In the case of this specific project, stakeholder groups included dealership employees, corporate headquarters employees, customers, the manufacturer, third-party suppliers, contractors working on the project, and the project team itself.

- **Divide and categorize.** The next step in the process is to try and get a handle on the needs of each of the stakeholder groups. Categorizing the stakeholders will also be a beneficial activity. The next chapter will focus in significantly greater depth on this topic.
- **Paint a picture.** Once there is a solid understanding of the business objectives of the project and each of the stakeholders and their needs have been identified, the team should begin to develop a narrative of the end point that is desired in the project. This is exactly like visioning sessions in strategy. What will help is asking the question "What will the future look like once the project is completed successfully?" This is really about trying to define the endpoint of the destination that the team is working toward. In our example, is it enough that the 10 locations are identified? Should we have a design for each location? Do we need to worry about furniture and layout? How about employees? Do we need to worry about hiring the employees at each of the location? How will we conduct transition from project activities to operational activities? All of these questions are important in trying to build the narrative for the destination or completion.
- **Establish the criteria.** Once there is clarity regarding the destination, the job of the project manager then should take all the information and build a robust set of success criteria that can be fed into a dashboard or a matrix

so that the customer may agree. The matrix can include items such as on-time delivery and within budget completion, along with specific details like punch-list detail being resolved and so forth.

- **Signoff.** Once the criteria are defined, it is important that the stakeholder groups, along with the client, sign off on this set of criteria. I have been in situations on projects where the exit criteria were defined but the client did not formally accept them. When it was time to conclude the project, the client did not sign on the deliverables, claiming that he never approved the exit criteria.

- **Closeout.** As I mentioned in previous chapters, one of the most important activities that will facilitate success is to conduct those closeout activities. A project that is not closed out is a project that is not complete. An incomplete activity is one that is not successful.

Documentation in this process becomes an important element for traceability. It would be greatly beneficial for your team to develop agreed-upon parameters for the following:

- **Project goal or vision:** This is a description of what the project is intended to achieve. The project vision is like a company vision—it should articulate the end state. However, what has to be understood by the team is that the project vision has to be aligned with the company vision. It is important to demonstrate here that the achievement of the project vision will ultimately help the company vision and strategy.

- **Project description:** This is a definition of the scope of the project. The team must be able to articulate what is going to be done on the project and what is not going to be done. Being able to scope out activities is as important as defining what will be done.

• **Project Objectives:** this is a list of each of the business objectives intended to be delivered upon completion of the project. However, this is not to be confused with the deliverables of the project. The purpose of identifying and listing objectives is that this will become the basis for the success exit criteria of the project.

Success Measures

It may be beneficial for your organization to develop a simple worksheet to allow the project team the ability to track performance from a completion perspective. Similar to the status report of project deliverables, this dashboard would focus on the business ends of the project. Table 12 is a sample template that can be used:

Project Objective	Measure	Target	Status
Increased customer loyalty	Repeat purchases	Within 3 months of initial purchase	Functionality under development
Revenue diversification	Sales generated from new products	5% of total revenue	Project completed, currently being tracked
Improved efficiency in accounting	Payment processing period	2 weeks	Achieved

Table 12. Sample template to track status of project objectives.

As I mentioned previously, the key to success is achieving a common definition and receiving the necessary buy in. Without common agreement, the project is likely to face insurmountable challenges during execution.

The biggest element to having consensus in defining success is agreement regarding the needs of the different stakeholders. This will be the subject of the upcoming chapter.

9

UNDERSTAND YOUR STAKEHOLDERS' NEEDS

"The key to failure is trying to please everybody."

Bill Cosby, Comedian, Actor, & Author

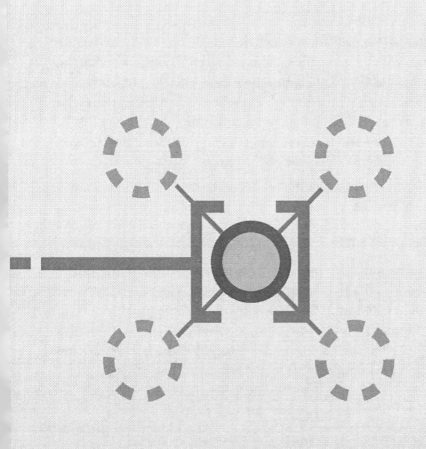

One project that I was given to manage some time ago in my career was a troubled project with a mid-sized organization. Our company had been contracted to help implement a "bleeding-edge" technology with the client. It seems that the customer at the time was unhappy with our company's performance on the project. During the initial debrief with the executive in charge of the project, he admitted that part of the problem had been the fact that the consulting team that was working on the project had too much turnover. The client had been "difficult." He also shared with me that our company had assigned one person to play both the architect role and the project manager role.

The challenge in this type of behavior is that it is almost absolutely impossible to both be a project manager and an IT architect. It's possible to play both roles, just not at the same time. Almost always, one role or the other is shortchanged, leaving the project floundering.

After going over the project documentation and conducting meetings with team members, I was ready to be introduced to the client organization. I thought I had done enough preparation to begin leading the team through the process of turning around the project. What shocked me more than anything was the fact that in this particular case the client really had no clue what they wanted out of this project. The client did not know their own needs.

Now it is one thing for the vendor or the consulting organization to not be familiar with the client needs, but for the organization to be unable to state their needs was a new experience for me. As I later learned, this is not that unusual in project management.

It turns out that so many organizations in the marketplace are not sure what they need out of a project. Customers, whether internal or external to the project team, are often unable to state their requirements because they don't know. I actually had a client once tell me "I am not sure what I want, but when I see it, I'll let you know."

The biggest problem with a lack of clarity around the needs of the client on a specific project is that this is a sure-fire way to guarantee confusion. The ability to identify the exact needs of a client organization, decipher them, prioritize them, and translate them into meaningful data points is fundamentally the cornerstone to building a successful project. It is indeed the foundation that allows the project manager to:

- Define project goals and objectives
- Establish the project scope and WBS,
- Create the project baseline and project management plan
- Manage issues and risks as they arise
- Identify critical success criteria for concluding the project effectively
- Deliver on time, within budget, and according to scope

A project manager who cannot facilitate the team in defining the organization's needs effectively is not going to be able to build the requirement needed to ensure proper execution. Furthermore, if the needs are not articulated effectively, it is harder to differentiate between product or service requirements versus project constraints.

One of the biggest challenges that project managers are faced with is trying to figure out which of the needs are actual needs versus wants in the organization. This may seem unimportant to those who are on the consulting side of the house because after all, what do you care if the item is a need or a want so long as the client pays for it?

That may be true: however, the moment the project faces trouble and the team is faced with the decision to change scope, adjust timelines, cut budgets, or replace resources, wouldn't it be nice to know which requirements are needs versus wants? This is particularly helpful in the small- and medium-sized organization setting, as any misstep on a project will not only cause potential project failure but indeed may threaten organizational sustainability.

Consider it this way. If your car had two components that were about to give out, which would you prefer that it be, the fan that cools down the radiator or the air conditioning fan? Both are desirable in running the car, however, if your aim is to go on a trip and reach your destination, only one type of fan is actually "needed" while the other one is desired.

In this chapter, we will discuss what project management practitioners need to consider as they build the foundation for effective planning and execution of their project, programs, and portfolios through managing needs and their expectations.

This is not necessarily a step-by-step approach to requirements management, as there are several books out there that help in doing so, but rather this is intended as a practical approach for small- and medium-sized business of the things that need to be taken into consideration in dealing with these issues.

Project Versus Product

It is very important in the initial stages of a project, prior to the initiation stage, to try and get a handle on the client's expectations of the project as opposed to the product/service that is being delivered in the project. The two types of needs are related but are actually quite different. The project manager should be able to differentiate, for instance, between a need to deliver project on a specific timeline to meet client revenue expectations versus the need to include certain functionality in the product of the project.

This activity is not only important from a scope perspective but also from a quality assurance perspective. Having a clear delineation between project needs versus product/service needs allows the team to develop different sets of control mechanisms throughout execution.

Doing so does not require rocket scientists, as it is a fairly simple process. In the needs-capturing phase, the project manager can categorize those into two categories then conduct a validation session with key stakeholders to ensure proper capture.

Deciphering Needs

Another important exercise that I mentioned earlier is to conduct dialogue sessions with key stakeholders to try and distinguish between needs and wants. Keep in mind that in most situations, clients and organizations may not be able to simply bucket something into the needs category versus the wants category.

The only way to actually get to the bottom of this is to go deeper into each of the needs. It requires that the project management practitioner ask lots of questions to establish a better and clearer understanding. One has to ask: Why this is functionality needed? Why is this deadline required? Can it be changed? Can it be delayed? Can it be ignored?

On one project that I managed while I was with IBM, the client told us from the beginning that there was a hard deadline that was specified by their client for the project and it was not possible to change it. We took their word for it and proceeded accordingly. It was not until months later that we discovered that the client actually had no idea that there was a willingness on their client's part to actually adjust the schedule. We only discovered this when the client came back to us to tell us that they needed additional functionality built into the solution. When we informed them that the added functionality would jeopardize the delivery date, they told us that it was okay because their client informed them that the date was not something set in stone!

I am not trying to advocate here that wants are not important: on the contrary, oftentimes wants are more important than needs. Sometimes you will find the reason your product sells in the marketplace is not so much that it meets a need but rather it meets a want.

The point that I am trying to make is that by understanding whether an item is a need or a want and project- versus product-related, the project team and the project manager are better prepared to deliver the project.

Pork-belly Projects

Before I delve too deeply into needs and requirements, there is another concept that is critical for managing needs and ultimately leading to project success. So often in organizations, individuals see that a project is getting ready to be approved and they rush to the project team with their needs in an attempt to add it to the list of things to be accomplished by the project or items to be delivered in the product.

In the U.S. Congress, one often sees this type of behavior when a bill is getting ready to be presented on the floor for a vote. Representatives from different districts around the country will tack on a specific expenditure to an important bill, thinking that by doing so they will get something for their constituency. Unfortunately, in too many instances they get their way because the bill is too important to shoot down and Congress is forced to vote for it.

This behavior in organizations can be detrimental because it often expands the scope so greatly and increases requirements into an unmanageable set. Project managers need to be able to develop a keen eye for unneeded requirements so as not to jeopardize the project.

From Needs and Into Requirements

Assuming that the project team has clarity around statements that can be categorized into wants versus needs, the project manager should be ready to begin the process of defining requirements for the project.

A requirement is an organizational need stated as a specification. It usually articulates a desired outcome, condition, or capability that should be met by the product or service that is being developed by the project. According to the *PMBOK® Guide*, a requirement should be documented and should be articulated quantitatively to reflect needs, wants, or expectations of stakeholders.

The one thing to keep in mind here is that if a requirement is not documented, communicated, and signed off on, then it is not a requirement. In fact, what distinguishes a good project manager from a great one is the ability to excel in the area of defining requirements and managing them throughout the project life cycle.

Levels of Complexity

In order to develop a healthy appreciation for requirements, one must understand that not all requirements are equal and similar. Requirements, in fact, exist at multiple levels. Project managers will often reach the conclusion that there are certain requirements that cannot be extracted until a higher-level set are first defined. In small- and medium-sized organizations this is particularly important because of the limited resources available to expend on change requests or rework. Clarity in requirements enables these types of organizations to mitigate against risks that threaten overall organizational sustainability.

For the purposes of most projects, requirements can be classified into three levels:

- **Business requirements:** These describe the needs and wants that must be met by the project at the organizational level. They could address issues that arise in processes, departments, legal matters, or financial performance dynamics

- **Functional requirements:** These are the components of the product and/or service of the project that must behave or act in a certain manner to meet the business needs of the organization.
- **Technical requirements:** These requirements are the specifications that will form the baseline for supporting the product and/or service of the project

For some individuals, reading the above description of each of the levels of requirements might be enough to help distinguish between them. However, for many people, the most practical way of understanding these levels of requirements is by offering a few examples in each of the categories.

Business requirements will often include statements such as these:

- We need a parking garage that will house 100 cars
- We need a 3 bedroom house
- We need an information system solution that allows us to better manage our customer relationships
- We want our new product to help us increase revenue by 30%
- The re-engineered process should allow us a 40% savings in cost

Functional requirements could be:

- The car should be able to drive 100 miles per hour
- The radio must have AM and FM frequencies
- The building must have an elevator that can handle 10 occupants
- The software must generate weekly project status reports
- The new system should be able to handle processing invoices

Technical requirements could be:

- The system must run on Linux
- The software must integrate with our Lotus Notes environment

- The car must run on unleaded gas
- The building must not have any asbestos
- The size of the pipes coming out of the house must be the same as those connecting to the sewage pipes

As demonstrated in the above examples, each of these requirements is important in their own right, but they each exist at a different level in the organization. Leading the team through a process that not only identifies them, but also classifies them accurately helps the project manager to develop a more holistic understanding of the total requirements.

The Iterative Approach

I mentioned earlier in the chapter that extracting requirements depends on the project team's ability to engage the different stakeholders in the organization to ensure that all of them are identified and no surprises emerge during implementation.

Another valid point is that requirements are not project elements that can be identified in one session, but rather are the product of significant dialogue among project team members. Adopting an iterative approach to extracting requirements is a critical success factor. Having the ability to review them multiple times and from multiple angles ensures that there is a higher level of accuracy in the result.

This will also prepare the project manager to better plan for the management of requirements once the project is in the implementation phase, as there is a need to demonstrate traceability and transparency in meeting those requirements.

Traceability

Those of us who have been involved in software development projects understand how important it is to demonstrate that the requirements were not only captured during the in beginning phases of initiation and planning, but also during delivery and change control.

Within IBM we had several templates that helped facilitate the extraction of and management of requirements. In fact, during my tenure at IBM, the organization acquired a company called Rational, which had an entire suite of products along with a methodology and a framework for managing requirements.

It may be unrealistic for your organization to deploy such sophisticated processes and products; however, there has to be clarity as to how the organization will approach traceability, otherwise it will be nearly impossible to close the project once all the deliverables have been submitted.

Business Process and Requirements

One excellent way that I have found to be extremely useful in extracting requirements is through documentation of as-is and to-be processes. I realize that I will not do this topic justice in this book; however, it is important enough for requirements that it is worth the mention.

Technology projects in particular, as well as any change efforts within the organization, require the project team to start the requirements definition process by developing process flow charts that define the as-is processes in the organization that will be impacted by the product and/or service.

In addition, the team needs to develop the to-be process model to help the organization understand how the process will look once the project is complete. A good benefit of building both as-is and to-be process documentation is the ability to identify the gap between the present and the future. This gap will be a great source for extracting requirements.

It is also important to understand that processes themselves in organizations exist at multiple levels. In change efforts that involve technology projects, these processes exist at the:

- Business level, simply describing the process flow. This process could be an accounts payable process or a vacation request process.
- Application level, describing how the functions of the system will impact the application and the flow within the system.
- Data level, describing how the actual data within the organization will flow from one database to another.

While this may seem irrelevant to non-technology projects, I have found that having a basic understanding may help project managers in the requirements management process.

From Requirements to Success

I had mentioned in the previous chapter that defining success cannot be achieved on projects ww clarity of requirements. Having a solid set of documented and approved requirements is indeed critical in projects. However, it is also important to lead the team through a prioritization process to help mitigate potential risks arising from delays in schedule or project overruns. This prioritization can take on a similar process to the one described in Chapter 6.

10

FOCUS ON THE BIG PICTURE

"Someone sent me a postcard picture
of the earth. On the back it said,
Wish you were here."

Steven Wright, Comedian, Actor, & Writer

Now that we have spent time discussing the importance of mastering the basics and leveraging the appropriate toolset to effectively manage projects, it is time to focus on the linkages outside of the project team and into the organization. The key to effective relationship-building outside of the project team is to remember that the big picture is more important than the detail. In addition it is also vital to strive for simplicity—less is more.

This is particularly relevant to small- and medium-sized organizations as it is not unusual that project team members are often assigned to multiple activities at the same time. They may be working on multiple projects or may have a functional responsibility along with project tasks. Additionally, project success or failure may have a greater impact on organizational performance because it may mean a life-or-death situation for the organization.

Seeing the Forest not the Trees

Having been associated with project management practitioners for so many years and understanding their mindset, I have come to a realization. Project management practitioners are great at managing change but, in many instances, focus too much on the details and ignore the big picture.

A joke that I often like to tell is about a friend who is also a project manager. When you ask him what time it is, he actually gives you a 30 minute lecture on how to build a clock. Sometimes it is necessary to step outside the project perspective and ensure that there is a solid understanding of the dynamics impacting the team's effort.

One challenge in performing in the role of project manager and working with project managers is that the same passion that helps us excel can also be a barrier to success. I have found myself, in certain situations, so focused on the needs that I had in managing the project that I ignored other dynamics in the organization.

When it comes to effectively leading the team, project management is like driving a car. The driver has to balance looking ahead too far with maintaining eye contact with the car immediately in front. Looking too far in advance while ignoring the object immediately ahead will cause an accident. Similarly, looking only immediately in front without paying attention to the distance will often cause the driver to miss exits or lose their way.

The great project management practitioner needs to be able to balance their ability to manage the details of the projects with the need to see the big picture. This is especially true because project practitioners can get distracted by tools and methodologies, templates and software programs, and standards and measurement. In small- and medium-sized businesses, there often is no safety net like in big organizations that allows for forgiveness when mistakes occur.

The Customer is Always Right

One of the things that I learned early on after I moved to the United States for my college studies is the importance of meeting and exceeding the needs of the customer. I was always amazed in service establishments by how much they go out of their way to assist the customer.

One story that I vividly remember from one of my business courses was a situation where a woman had bought tires for her car. Apparently she did not like the tires because of how they felt while driving. She decided to go return them. However, instead of going to Sears, the store that likely sold the tires, she ended up going to Bloomingdale's.

Interestingly enough, when the sales clerk saw her, he recognized her as a regular customer. He welcomed her to the store and asked her how he could help. She explained that she wanted to return the tires. He accompanied her to the parking lot, saw the tires and went back into the store. He issued her a refund and took the tires. The surprise in this story is not so much that the sales clerk paid a refund against the company policy without a sales receipt. The amazing thing is that Bloomingdale's does not even sell tires! He had gone out of his way in support of the customer's needs and desires. The customer in this case was totally wrong, but the clerk recognized that it was in his power to help and he felt empowered to do so.

I often relate this story to participants of my workshops as an example of maintaining focus on the needs of the customers, not just simply what the company can or cannot do. Sadly, however, the business world and service establishments are moving away from this attitude of service for customers.

I was in a situation recently at a restaurant where the waiter totally ignored my order because he lacked effective listening skills. When I pointed out that it might be good to listen to the customers, he started arguing with me that it was not his fault that my order was not right. He started blaming all sorts of other individuals including the cook, the person who punched the order into the system, and even the restaurant manager.

It is easy in service establishments to recognize when our needs are met or if our wants are ignored. Sometimes however, when we are working in project settings within various corporate cultures, the point is lost on us. I suspect that some readers are, in fact, thinking—what does the above story have to do with project management?

Sadly, project management standards and books don't focus enough on this issue. Project management practitioners, in essence, exist to satisfy the needs of customers. Customer service is at the heart of our focus.

One experience that I had managing a project back in the mid 1990s is particularly appropriate. At the time I was brought into a client organization specifically because of my project management knowledge, industry experience, and functional understanding of the specific project. I remember feeling so arrogant because I knew that the customer needed me. I felt like a hot-shot project manager with a huge amount of power and authority. Even though I working as a consultant on the client site, I had significantly greater influence on client executives than most employees did. My project executive sponsor was one of the vice presidents in the IT organization. I was effectively working with this individual to deliver a project for their client organization in the business development area.

In the initial stages of the project, I believe that I did a good job building rapport with the project team and different stakeholders. I also developed a good friendship with the executive in the business development area and found that the two of us worked well as a team.

As we concluded the process of requirements definition and vendor selection, we began the project planning cycle to get ready for implementation. The team had done an amazing job in selecting the right vendor for the job. I was feeling pretty smug in my ability to lead this team and get them corralled in the right way.

However, right before the commencement of execution we encountered a problem with a department head who was a peer of my colleague in business development. It seems that after he reviewed our implementation plan, he was unhappy with the fact that the solution was going to be deployed in his department last.

He then proceeded to conduct a series of political maneuvers in the organization and threatened to go to the marketing vice president if my colleague did not change the deployment order. My colleague from business development folded under pressure and agreed to accommodate this department head's request, even though it was not in the best interest of the company, the project, and the users.

During a team meeting to conduct the final review of the deployment schedule, my business development colleague communicated to the team that not only will we need to change the order of deployment, but that there were additional requirements coming from this department head that will cause a delay in the schedule.

After extensive team deliberations, the discussion became more heated. At one point, and in the heat of the argument, I basically made some comments that clearly undermined my business development colleague's authority. The meeting concluded with my colleague feeling ridiculed because of the way I responded. My reaction appeared as though I was highlighting an incompetence, which was not deserved.

This colleague then proceeded immediately to the IT vice president's office to complain about my behavior. While the IT vice president had seen the value of what I had done for the client organization and liked me a lot, there was no choice but to release me from the consulting engagement. After all, I was a consulting resource and the other party was an executive in the company.

As I reflect on this memory, I realize that my actions were wrong. It was not that I was unprofessional. The issue was that I had challenged someone's authority without keeping in mind that they were the customer. In fact, I was no different from that waiter who told me that it was not his fault that my order was wrong.

The problem that the team was presented with was not one that I caused. Its solution was also out of my hands; however, in that moment when I had a lapse in judgment and ignored the mantra "the customer is always right," I lost the engagement.

The most valuable lesson that I learned in my project management career happened in this situation. I learned that it is possible to win an argument but end up losing anyway. The primary loser in this whole exercise was me.

Had I simply worked with the team, we might have been able to get past our frustrations and resolved the issue in a manner that preserved the integrity of the project, while at the same time dealing with the political dynamics of the organization.

There will come a point in every project manager's career where pragmatism will be more important than idealism. Project management is as much an art as it is a science—practitioners need to remember that in dealing with stakeholders.

Quality is a Must

Another area that is ignored, often to the determent of projects, is quality. In most of my project teams throughout the years, I find that this is a subject that very few people understand. This lack of understanding often leads to simple confusion. Some project managers come to believe that if there is a need to shorten the duration of the project or manage cost, there has to be flexibility in terms of achieving quality parameters on the project.

In my early years managing information technology projects, it was not unusual for the project team to ignore product quality all together. The team simply thought that there will always be defects that need fixing, so why bother with defining quality parameters? They simply assumed that they could deal with them later.

Others confuse quality with grade. This is also another erroneous view of quality. If I had to rely on a good description of quality, it would be that quality is the product and/or service performing in a manner that meets the specification and design. Grade, on the other hand, speaks more of "bells and whistles." Let's take the example of automobiles. A Mercedes-Benz S-class car is a relatively large and expensive luxury. On the other hand, a Honda Civic is a small economy car that is significantly cheaper.

These cars are very different in shape, style, size, function, and so forth, yet they both meet the definition of "car." They both have engines and they both fulfill the function of transportation. However, they are each a different grade of car. The difference in shape, style, and so on, means that the cost is different—however, the quality may be the same. Consider the reaction if

Honda Motor Company issued a statement that said "Since the Civic is so much cheaper than the Mercedes-Benz, we will not include an engine or a roof." How silly would this sound?

The bottom line is that while grade on projects can be reduced to manage timeline and cost, quality is not something that should be sacrificed. Unfortunately, many projects suffer with quality problems because they do not plan for quality effectively. The other challenge is that quality is sometimes less tangible and is viewed as a matter of perspective. As a result, it becomes harder to manage.

My favorite story describing quality comes from a training session I attended in the late 1990s. The instructor told us that one challenge that people have with quality is that they do not set the proper expectations. When one goes to a garage to get a car problem fixed, the mechanic might tell them that he does not know the cost of the repair and as a result, when the job is done, the client is not happy.

He then shared a story of an experience that he had with his car. He said that one morning he was getting ready to go to work when his car did not start. He called the garage and they sent a tow truck to take the car to the mechanic. Upon inspection, the mechanic called the instructor back to inform him of the exact problem.

In addition to describing the way he was going to fix the car, the mechanic proceeded to provide a specific timeline and an exact cost of the repair. On the day that the car was supposed to be ready after the repair was completed, our instructor got a call from the mechanic. He had expected the mechanic to tell him that the car was not ready. However, he was surprised to learn that the car was ready. When he went to pick it up, he was further surprised to find out that not only did the mechanic fix the car the exact way he described, but also that the cost of the repair was exactly as he had originally promised.

Now, for most of us, having experienced such an event, we would be ecstatic. The "project" was delivered within scope, on time, and within budget. What more could we ask for? Sadly, however, our instructor informed us that he was not happy with the job the mechanic did. He then asked us "Why do you think I was unhappy when the car was working perfectly, it was done on time, and it cost exactly as promised?

I must admit that this story is so good that I have used it for many of my workshops. However, in all the years that I have used it, I had yet to hear someone provide the right answer.

As it turns out, when our instructor went to pick up the car, he had an important business meeting so he was dressed in a nice suit with tie and white shirt. After he had paid for the garage bill he got into the car and behind the steering wheel. The moment he put the car in gear and began to drive, he looked down and saw a huge black grease stain on his white shirt. That not only ruined the shirt, but it also meant that his business meeting was going to either be delayed or he would look silly going to it with grease on his shirt. Sadly, the mechanic forgot to inspect the car on the inside to ensure that there were no grease stains before he delivered "his project."

The beauty of this simple story is that it demonstrates so clearly how easy it is for project teams to forget about quality and assume that just because they deliver a product or service their job is done.

This is yet another area that leaders implementing project management practices in their organizations need to pay attention to so as to ensure that project teams address it effectively.

Embrace Excellence and Be Realistic

Perhaps one way to ensure that quality is addressed effectively is to ensure that project management practitioners hired into the organization are individuals who do not aspire to mediocrity.

This is something that I must admit often surprises me in developing countries. Perhaps there is a skills gap that does not allow small- and medium-sized companies in such economies to hire the best and the brightest. However, I have seen first-hand many examples of people who are comfortable with not achieving the best results and accepting second best.

Embracing excellence, as I mentioned earlier in the book, is a critical leadership skill that is needed to achieve success. Without having this mentality as a cornerstone in building the project management framework in the organization, leaders will face significant challenges.

The flip side of this attitude, however, is trying to take on too much in the organization. Sometimes executives think that if they start several initiatives all at the same time, they are "lighting a fire" under people and putting pressure on them to perform. I used to have a manager who said "pressure makes diamonds." While this, at face value, may make sense, unfortunately if the organization takes on too many projects at once, resources will lack the necessary focus to deliver properly, and it becomes likely that projects will fight over these limited resources. The net result will be chaos at best.

Unfortunately, there is no magic number that is prescribed in terms of the number of initiatives that an organization can take on. This will greatly depend on the organization. Some can only handle one large project at a time, while others may have the capability to take on five. One has to account for a bit of trial and error to get this right, unless there are realistic individuals who are familiar with the organization and who are willing to advise the project practitioners.

Neutralize those Buzzwords

My involvement in PMI had exposed me to a new way of thinking. It also opened many doors for me professionally. However, what I did not count on was also becoming familiar with so many buzzwords and TLAs. TLA stands for three-letter acronyms.

Project management practitioners become masters in creating new acronyms. While I have not counted them, I am willing to bet that the *PMBOK® Guide* must have over 100 acronyms describing tools, methods, techniques, and concepts. This ranges from the simplest WBS to the more complex ETC (estimate to complete).

I later discovered that if project managers had mastered acronyms, IBM must have invented them. I had seen so many meetings where entire conversations were dominated by TLAs. We often forget that when we introduce the concepts of project management to small- and medium-sized organizations there is little familiarity with the language of projects. As a result, rather than simplify things, we find ourselves fighting a war of words.

I remember an incident in one company I worked in where an argument took place related to job titles. The person who was championing the establishment of the new project management office wanted to hire "project managers." He was going over a presentation describing why the company needed more "project managers" when another executive said that he did not like the word "manager." He said let's call them "leader" instead of manager because this way it would be less likely to anger the functional managers in the organization.

Whatever your choice of words might be or the latest trend in buzzwords ranging from reengineering to lean Six Sigma, the bottom line is this. If the executive team does not successfully establish a common language for project management, there will be troubles ahead.

Being able to have a common lexicon to refer to ideas and concepts ensures a greater level of acceptability and accountability on projects.

Sidestep the Methodology

I have discussed the issue of methodology in several sections of the book. However, I believe that there is an important nugget of wisdom that needs to be shared to help project management practitioners focus on the forest rather than the trees.

A methodology is not intended to help an organization entangle the project managers in endless fights and confuse the project team during the delivery. If it becomes apparent that the organization is having an all-out fight over the methodology, the solution is very simple.

Don't have one.

As I had articulated earlier in the book, project management is about people first. If there is a strong team in charge of managing projects and taking control of initiatives, then they need to be experienced enough to not need a step-by-step methodology with a full set of tools along-side it.

The more experience I develop in project management, the less use I have for methodologies and tools. Having a template created in Excel can be just as good as having very expensive software that can spit out a risk mitigation plan.

Structures

Another pitfall that project management practitioners fall into, especially in small- and medium-sized organizations is the notion of organizational structures as a means to achieving success in deploying project management.

I have often been in discussions where someone would say "But our organizational structure does not allow us to manage projects effectively." I will grant them that it is true that structure can be a barrier, but having a "projectized" environment is not a panacea for project management either.

One client that I have worked with was extremely worried that their structure was not optimal. He spent months engaging other executives in discussion over how to re-organize the management hierarchy in a way to achieve greater success in the company. It took a lot to try and convince him that there is no such thing as a perfect structure. This is especially difficult for engineering types who happen to make up a large portion of the project management community.

During my MBA studies I learned that Henry Ford was an idealist. He believed that there was such a thing as the perfect car. The joke that he often told about his model T car was, "you can have it in any color you want, so long as it is black."

In most of my encounters with project management practitioners, it seems that there is often a false assumption that project management cannot come of age without the existence of a PMO. They assume that if the official organizational chart recognizes the existence of such a department and hires a functional manager for it, that demonstrates the level of commitment needed to have influence in the company.

While it is true that PMOs may bring a great deal of benefit to the organization, the reality of the matter is that I have yet to hear of a single company that went out of business because they did not have a PMO. In tough times, in fact, often the first thing that goes out the door, along with the training budget, is the PMO budget.

For small- and medium-sized businesses, there may not be enough of a justification to build a PMO to support project management. However, that could very well be the topic of a whole different book.

This does not mean that there should not be a champion for the practice of project management. It also does not mean that there is no need for project management and standards. I am simply stating that PMOs are only a means to an end, the end being great project management practice leading to effective implementation of strategic projects. The end is definitely not having a lot of organizational power and authority.

Fire the Cynics, or at Least Avoid Them

The last piece of advice I can offer in terms of striving for simplicity is that nothing kills innovation, energy, creativity, drive, and passion more quickly than cynicism. There is no room for cynics in organizations striving for excellence. If there is one thing that must be done before any framework, methodology, and practice can be implemented, it is to get rid of those cynics in the organization.

Some may come back and say that the problem is that the CEO or the owner of the company is the cynic. The best advice I can give in this case is to dust off that old résumé and begin that job search!

CONCLUSION

"Finish each day and be done with it. You have done what you could. Some blunders and absurdities no doubt crept in; forget them as soon as you can. Tomorrow is a new day; begin it well and serenely and with too high a spirit to be encumbered with your old nonsense."

Ralph Waldo Emerson, American Poet

What's Important

When I first set out to write this book, I had envisioned an easy-to-follow outline that can be practical enough for the busy executive engaged in leading small- and medium-sized organizations. My intent was to try and make project management a bit more relevant for these organizations beyond simply reading the *PMBOK® Guide*.

As I look at some of the more important items as a leave-behind, I want to highlight the following:

- Business goals and objectives are the reason for undertaking any project. The project management practitioner should never lose sight of that.
- Satisfying client needs in a proactive and partnership manner is critical not only to success but also to employee satisfaction.
- Project management is a discipline that facilitates delivery, and, as such, project managers must be action-oriented and results-focused.
- There is a huge difference between good practice and fancy tools. Remember, a fool with a tool is just a fool.
- It would be wise to remember that every small- and medium-sized organization has limited resources and bandwidth. It's better not to expect too much in way of expenditure of financial resources on deploying project management methodology.
- Keep in mind that there is no cookie-cutter approach to designing, launching, and building your project management framework. It has to be tailored to your organization.

Nuggets of Wisdom

In addition to maintaining focus on what's important, there are a few "to dos" that the project manager at the small- and medium-sized business should initiate almost immediately after they start. These include:

- **Connecting through language.** Establishing a common lexicon for terminology in the organization.
- **Building or operating.** Sometimes you must ignore building the methodology and focus on managing transformation.
- **Bridging the gap.** Building a connection into the organization as a whole even if the structure is not conducive to the practice of project management.
- **Indoctrinating the people.** Educating the organization as to the effective practice of project management. Sometimes you have to be a trainer.
- **Creating common ground.** Building consensus and trying to gain the buy-in of influential people in the organization. It would also be good not to alienate people who might be predisposed to supporting you.
- **Advancing the leaders.** Developing a career path— even an informal one—by mentoring and coaching to grow the project management practice within the company.
- **Solving the real problem.** It is critical that project management practitioners spend time on identifying true causes of a problem in order to address it effectively. Often I have seen practitioners blind-sided with the glitter of automation, which makes them believe that any organizational can be solved by applying automation to it. Automation may be a good option to assist in addressing issues, but often there are causes buried deep that require focus before automation is applied.

Best-Practices Review

I suspect that one can write an entire book filled with nothing more but tons of bullet points with key best practices that the project management professional should follow. Having run out of space and time, here are a few for consideration.

- **Requirements.** Specifications are critical in defining success and establishing clarity of business objectives.
- **People.** Make sure that project managers have strong business acumen, not just a technical understanding of project management or a technical field.
- **Flexibility.** There is not one way of doing things, there are multiple ways and many methodologies.
- **Head Start.** Establish some quick wins so that success can come early. This way, you can leverage your track record in transforming attitudes and winning employees over.
- **Politics.** Do not ignore corporate dynamics and politics— you do so at your own peril.
- **Focus.** Be strategic in orientation and detailed in action.

Lessons Learned

Having been in the field for many years, I have learned some hard lessons. I hope that my lessons can help you avoid my mistakes so that you can make many of your own.

- **Prioritize.** Don't become blindsided by all the organizational problems outside of the scope of the project. Don't get pulled into them.
- **Collaborate.** Figure out who's with you and who's against you. Keeping your enemies close may be a drag, but at least find out who they are.
- **Optimize.** Work on getting rid of the ineffective resources. You may not have enough authority to fire them, but at least keep them away from your projects.
- **Eliminate.** Don't be afraid to say no to non-value-adding activities if you are presented the opportunity.
- **Be grounded.** Be optimistic but realistic. Make sure that the schedule includes risk contingencies.

- **Achieve.** Show visible progress and success to the executive sponsor, or they will become bored and change direction on you.
- **Support.** Try to make the executives look good. Otherwise, they might bounce you out of the organization.
- **Simplify.** Don't establish overcomplicated processes. Strive to break things down.

It's all Made Up

An old mentor of mine used to say project managers often take themselves too seriously. He asked why they overcomplicate things, especially since it's all made up. None of it exists naturally in the environment, otherwise you'd see scope creep on the road.

While project management conceptually can be complex, executing projects in small- and medium-sized organizations does not have to be. If there is proper understanding of the expectations and proper leadership on the project team, these conditions can help simplify the overall approach.

Please remember that project management is not the end goal, it is the means by which an organization can help achieve success and deliver on its promises.